Going Tactile

OXFORD STUDIES IN THE ANTHROPOLOGY OF LANGUAGE

Series editor: Alessandro Duranti, *University of California at Los Angeles*

This series is devoted to works from a wide array of scholarly traditions that treat linguistic practices *as* forms of social action.

Editorial Board
Patricia Baquedano-Lopez, *University of California, Berkeley*
Donald Brenneis, *University of California at Santa Cruz*
Paul B. Garrett, *Temple University*
Janet McIntosh, *Brandeis University*
Justin Richland, *University of California, Irvine*

Thank You for Dying for Our Country: Commemorative Texts and Performances in Jerusalem
Chaim Noy

Singular and Plural: Ideologies of Linguistic Authority in 21st Century Catalonia
Kathryn A. Woolard

Linguistic Rivalries: Tamil Migrants and Anglo-Franco Conflicts
Sonia Neela Das

The Monologic Imagination
Edited by Matt Tomlinson and Julian Millie

Looking Like a Language, Sounding Like a Race: Raciolinguistic Ideologies and the Learning of Latinidad
Jonathan Rosa

Talking Like Children: Language and the Production of Age in the Marshall Islands
Elise Berman

The Struggle for a Multilingual Future: Youth and Education in Sri Lanka
Christina P. Davis

The Last Language on Earth: Linguistic Utopianism in the Philippines
Piers Kelly

Rethinking Politeness with Henri Bergson
Edited by Alessandro Duranti

Other Indonesians: Nationalism in an Unnative Language
Joseph Errington

Recognizing Indigenous Languages: Double Binds of State Policy and Teaching Kichwa in Ecuador
Nicholas Limerick

Going Tactile: Life at the Limits of Language
Terra Edwards

Going Tactile

Life at the Limits of Language

Terra Edwards

OXFORD
UNIVERSITY PRESS

Oxford University Press is a department of the University of Oxford.
It furthers the University's objective of excellence in research, scholarship,
and education by publishing worldwide. Oxford is a registered trade mark of
Oxford University Press in the UK and in certain other countries.

Published in the United States of America by Oxford University Press
198 Madison Avenue, New York, NY 10016, United States of America.

© Oxford University Press 2024

All rights reserved. No part of this publication may be reproduced,
stored in a retrieval system, or transmitted, in any form or by any means,
without the prior permission in writing of Oxford University Press,
or as expressly permitted by law, by license or under terms agreed with
the appropriate reprographics rights organization. Inquiries concerning
reproduction outside the scope of the above should be sent to
the Rights Department, Oxford University Press, at the address above.

You must not circulate this work in any other form and you must impose this same condition on any acquirer

Library of Congress Cataloging-in-Publication Data

Names: Edwards, Terra, author.
Title: Going tactile : life at the limits of language / Terra Edwards.
Description: New York, NY : Oxford University Press, 2024. |
Series: Oxford studies in the anthropology of language | Includes bibliographical references and index.
Identifiers: LCCN 2024000732 (print) | LCCN 2024000733 (ebook) |
ISBN 9780197778029 (hardback) | ISBN 9780197778036 (paperback) | ISBN 9780197778050 (epub)
Subjects: LCSH: Deafblind people—United States.
Classification: LCC HV1597 .E393 2024 (print) | LCC HV1597 (ebook) |
DDC 362.4/10973—dc23/eng/20240311
LC record available at https://lccn.loc.gov/2024000732
LC ebook record available at https://lccn.loc.gov/2024000733

Contents

Acknowledgments   vii

1. Life at the Limits of Language   1
  1.1 How to Read This Book   2
    1.1.1 Translation, Style, and Convention   6
  1.2 This Is a Jar Containing Strawberry Jam   10
  1.3 Residence in the World   15
    1.3.1 Affordances   16
    1.3.2 Direct Perception   18
  1.4 Representations of the World   20
    1.4.1 Metatactile Knowledge   23
    1.4.2 Language Emergence   26
  1.5 Life at the Limits of Language   30
  1.6 Conclusion   34

2. Creating DeafBlind Identity   35
  2.1 Building a Bridge   40
  2.2 "We Need Interpreters"   42
  2.3 DeafBlind Identity   46

3. The Collapse of the World   48
  3.1 Embracing DeafBlind Identity   53
  3.2 What Identity Obscures   56
  3.3 Existential Strain   59
  3.4 Commitment Issues   64
  3.5 Keeping Things Life-Like   69
  3.6 Signs of Collapse   73

4. The Protactile Movement   75
  4.1 "Everything We Touched Froze"   77
  4.2 "The Family Was Almost Dead"   79
  4.3 When the Problem Is the Solution   85
  4.4 Learning about the World   87
  4.5 Motivating Action   89
  4.6 Re-defining Roles   92
  4.7 Going Tactile   94
  4.8 Conclusion   101

5. Being for Speaking   103
  5.1 Thinking for Speaking   104
  5.2 Ways of Being DeafBlind   107

vi Contents

5.3 New Ways of Being "Tactile"	109
5.4 Being for Speaking	111
5.5 Conclusion	118

6. The Laminated Environment — **120**
- 6.1 Deaf Space — 121
  - 6.1.1 Urban Development — 121
  - 6.1.2 Participation — 122
  - 6.1.3 Imagination — 125
- 6.2 Being Protactile in Deaf Space — 127
  - 6.2.1 "Where Am I Now?" — 128
  - 6.2.2 Affordances in Deaf Space — 130
  - 6.2.3 The Laminated Environment — 133
- 6.3 Conclusion — 135

7. Conclusions — **137**

References — 141
Index — 146

Acknowledgments

This book is the product of years of conversations with mentors, peers, students, and colleagues, and could not have been completed without support from my family and friends. My deepest thanks to everyone in the Seattle DeafBlind community, who invited me into their lives, spent time with me, and shared their stories. In particular, I am grateful to my teacher, friend, and colleague Jelica B. Nuccio. I met Jelica when I was an undergraduate student just learning to communicate, and she whipped me into shape. We went on to become close collaborators and her influence on my life and this work has been profound. I am also grateful to aj granda for the many conversations and provocations to think about the problems central to this book. Theresa B. Smith, Shawn Broderick, and Ellie Savidge were key figures in my education who painted vivid and compelling pictures of the historical, social, and political dynamics at play in Deaf and DeafBlind communities, which continue to animate my work to this day. I am especially grateful to Theresa Smith for introducing me to the field of linguistic anthropology, for long conversations about language and culture, and for her encouragement and guidance in conducting this research. I am deeply indebted to the members of the Seattle DeafBlind community who participated in this research, the people who offered feedback and encouragement as I learned the language and interpreting skills that made this research possible, and those who shared their memories of the history of the community, as well as their newspaper clippings, notes, boxes of old newsletters, and other critical materials analyzed in this book. I must also thank Vince Nuccio, who has contributed to this work in far too many ways for me to list here, and who has remained a valued friend and interlocutor throughout.

There are several people who contributed to this work as it expanded to include the effects of the protactile movement in Washington, D.C. Robert T. Sirvage and Hansel Bauman let me tag along for months, use their hard hats, look at their blueprints, and generally take up their time. My thinking has changed course as a result of all they taught me. Thank you to Liz Brading, Oscar Chacon, Darla Konkel, Eddie Martinez, Sarah McMillen, Yashaira Romilus, and the participants of the Tactile Mind Collaborative for the stimulating conversations, insights, and collaborations during my time in D.C. I am also grateful to the DeafBlind community members, architects, planners, administrators, and other practitioners of Deaf Space design who participated in this research. Chapter 6 also benefited from discussions at the Theorizing Deaf Geographies workshop at Heriot-Watt University in Edinburgh, hosted by Amandine le Maire, Sanchayeeta Iyer, Annelies Kusters, and Erin Moriarty Harrelson. In addition to the organizers, Dai O'Brien, Joseph Murray, and Mike Gulliver all gave me helpful feedback and shared important insights.

Two individuals who have had a significant effect on my thinking and the arguments presented in this book in various places: the DeafBlind poet, essayist, and researcher, John Lee Clark, whose hands flutter, and Halene Anderson, whose big ideas land with a gentle touch. Their influence crept up on me in the years leading up to the publication of this book and our ongoing dialogue has sustained me in the writing process.

I am grateful to my mentors and colleagues in the places where I studied and worked as this project was taking shape. William F. Hanks, my advisor and mentor at Berkeley, weighed in on countless essays, articles, and presentations over the years, introduced me to many of the conceptual frameworks needed to pursue the questions I address in this book, and has been a source of unwavering support as I have begun to find my own way as a scholar. I also left Berkeley with a supportive group of peers and colleagues whom I have been turning to for advice and guidance ever since, especially Joshua Craze, Michele Friedner, E. Mara Green, Bharat Jayram Venkat, Shaylih Muehlmann, and Xochitl Marsilli-Vargas.

I am tremendously thankful for my colleagues in the Department of Comparative Human Development at the University of Chicago, who are supportive, kind, and brilliant. I have come to depend on the quick and insightful feedback that Marisa "Middy" Casillas is willing to give on just about everything I write. I am also grateful for her friendship and the snacks she brings to work. Eugene Raikhel has generously offered his time as a mentor and colleague since my arrival at the University of Chicago, and our conversations have inspired new directions in my thinking. When things fell apart (just as this book was supposed to be coming together), Eman Abdelhadi, Marisa Casillas, Jennifer Cole, Michele Friedner, and Chiara Galli were there for me as colleagues and as friends. I have also benefited immensely from Diane Brentari's wisdom and intellect as a co-author, co-teacher, co-director, and mentor. Sections of this book were written during our co-taught seminar, "New Perspectives on Language Emergence" taught at the University of Chicago in the fall of 2023 and our collaborations have informed the linguistic analyses presented in the book. My colleagues in Saint Louis also helped shape this book, especially Monica Eppinger, with whom I was in dialogue as the framework for this book was coming together. Amy Cooper and Talia Dan-Cohen each gave excellent feedback on one of the chapters at just the right moment. Finally, thank you to the Linguistics Department at Gallaudet for their support as I conducted this research, especially Paul Dudis, whose questions always kept me thinking in new ways about the relationship between language and context, and to several colleagues who were or had been at Gallaudet who became valued friends and important sources of support, including Deborah Chen-PIchler, Paul Dudis, Joseph Hill, Julie Hochgesang, Ceil Lucas, Deborah Peterson, Miako Rankin, and Emily Shaw. I would never have made it to this point without them.

My fellow linguistic anthropologists have given me generous feedback at conferences, workshops, invited talks, and classes. Special thanks to Constantine Nakassis, who has organized numerous workshops, reading groups, and conferences, all of which have been important venues that have shaped my thinking during the final stages of writing this book. Thanks to Constantine and the co-organizers and participants in the metasemiotics club at the University of Chicago; participants in the Design Ideologies workshop, hosted by Constantine Nakassis and Jürgen Spitzmüller, and funded by the University of Chicago, especially Susan Gal, Keith Murphy, Kamala Russell, and Lily Ye, who provided feedback on the final substantive chapter of the book. The participants in John Lee Clark's Protactile Theory seminar have shared critical insights over the years. Benjamin Lee, Greg Urban, and the members of the Semiotics Group at the Center for Transcultural Studies, especially William Hanks, Miyako Inoue, Paul Kockelman, Kamala Russell, and Kathleen Stewart provided encouragement, inspiration, and provocation and I am grateful for their influence on this work. Greg Urban also gave me detailed comments on portions of the manuscript that were immensely helpful.

Thank you to Alessandro Duranti for his editorial guidance from start to finish and for his warmth and encouragement along the way. Thanks to Chuck Goodwin for encouraging Sandro and I to work together and for his unflagging support, even when this book was just an idea. The editorial staff at Oxford University Press has also been extremely helpful, including Meredith Keffer, Emily Benitez, Julia Steer and Ponneelan Moorthy, as well as two anonymous reviewers, and thank you to Bob Offer-Westort for his unusual and discerning ability to analyze and evaluate book indexes, and for creating this book's index.

This research was supported by the Wenner-Gren Foundation for Anthropological Research (Grant #8110 and Grant #9146), the National Science

Foundation's Linguistics program (BCS-1651100), and Gallaudet University's Priority Research grant. The writing phase was supported by funding from Saint Louis University's Research Institute.

Since the beginning of my graduate training, I have lived in many cities where I have been lucky to find friends, often fellow parents, who kept me sane, made me laugh, and helped me put things into perspective. I'm especially grateful for Denecia Billups, David Downing, Kira Hunter, Felicia and Marius Ionescu, Ebeth Johnson, Kahreen Tebeau, and Cristina Trevizo.

Last but not least, thank you to my parents, Greg and Lorri Edwards, for their love, support, and patience, and for encouraging me to pursue what I love even when it didn't make very much sense. And thank you to my son, Isaac Redfield who, with all of his unimaginably lovable intersubjective idiosyncrasies, reminds me to appreciate life in new ways every day and inspires me with his determination and commitment to his own passions. I am lucky to have a son like him.

1
Life at the Limits of Language

This book is about the limits of language, life after collapse, and what it means to find new ways of being in the world. It distills nearly 20 years of anthropological engagement with DeafBlind people in the United States, many of whom acquired American Sign Language, or ASL, as their first language, attended Deaf schools, were involved in Deaf organizations, and had Deaf friends and partners. Due to a shared genetic condition called Usher Syndrome, they slowly became blind over the course of many years. As that process unfolded, the visual world they once knew collapsed, and for many it was not clear how life could continue. Starting in the late 1970s, this problem was addressed with increasing dependence on sighted interpreters. At first, as the process of becoming blind was just beginning, interpreters relayed messages via ASL. As time went on, more of the world needed to be relayed, until eventually descriptions of the world were expected to stand in for the world itself.

The main claim at the heart of this book is that the collapse of the world was not a result of becoming blind but rather the culmination of many years of substituting statements about the world for the world. Although we can be carried away into the world of a novel, or struck by the vividness of a friend's story, it is not possible to live in a description when the description is all you have. In other words, there is a limit to what language can do when the world is falling apart and existence itself is at stake. I am not claiming that language, in some universal sense, is deficient or unimportant. The claim is that there are existential conditions that must be in place in order for language to be effective as a means of talking about, or representing, the world.

The book focuses on a particular historical moment in two DeafBlind communities (one in Seattle, Washington, and one in Washington, D.C.), where DeafBlind people were trying to find new ways of being in the world and as part of that process found themselves grappling with the limits of language. In the 1990s, two DeafBlind leaders in Seattle took a novel approach. They claimed that descriptions of the world, filtered through sighted interpreters, were largely unnecessary, since all human activity could be carried out through touch. With their community, they sought new tactile ways of communicating, interacting, and navigating. This effort became the "protactile movement," and it spread quickly across the country. Reporting on more than 30 months of fieldwork with DeafBlind political leaders, artists, educators, and community members, this book tells the story of what I learned about the limits of language as the DeafBlind people I knew were, as they said, "going tactile."

1.1 How to Read This Book

How you read this book will depend on who you are. If you are DeafBlind, you may wonder what a hearing, sighted person such as myself can possibly offer. My answer is that DeafBlind communities, organizations, and individuals will offer far more than I can. However, over the course of nearly 20 years of research, many of my friends, colleagues, and acquaintances have become DeafBlind, and I have listened to them carefully as they shared their experiences. I have also studied the history of the institutions that shaped those experiences and spent time observing, first hand, the emergence of radically new options for how a person could be DeafBlind. It is my hope that the analysis of those changes presented in this book will deter readers who are DeafBlind, their family, friends, and others in their communities from thinking about blindness itself as the cause of issues at work, communication breakdown, or problems in relationships. By the end, I hope these readers are convinced that these problems are not "in" any one individual but distributed across groups of people, institutions, infrastructure, and the environment as a whole.

What became known as the protactile movement did not begin as a set of established practices or rules to be learned. It started by finding protected places, where dominant sighted norms could be suspended and new and more tactile ways of being could be discovered. In those places, blame and frustration shifted from the individual, their biological development, and their psychological ability to cope to the social, historical, and political processes that obscured tactile affordances in the first place. Finding a way forward from there was a collective project, which sighted people have had little to contribute to. Unlike DeafBlind people in the past, you will now find organized political efforts led by and for DeafBlind people. As DeafBlind writer John Lee Clark says, "It's an exciting time to be DeafBlind" (2014).

For interpreters, teachers, family members, and friends, I hope this book will help you step back and consider the broader social and historical processes that have made the role you currently have available to you, and think about what function that role has within larger systems. When I was socialized into the Seattle DeafBlind community in the late 1990s, almost a decade before the inception of the protactile movement, sighted people had a much more central role. As an undergraduate student interested in language and communication, I moved to Seattle to start training to become an interpreter. Over the next four years, I became increasingly involved in the DeafBlind community. I was employed at a restaurant owned by a DeafBlind man and staffed by Deaf and DeafBlind employees; I regularly attended social and community events; I had DeafBlind friends and roommates; and I was tentatively trying out the role of interpreter. By the time I completed my undergraduate education, I was embedded in the community and had internalized many local standards and norms for interaction and communication. As students of interpreting, we were taught that DeafBlind people are at risk of social isolation, so when sighted people are around they should try to do all they can to provide useful and interesting information that can help maintain some connection to the world.

Shortly after I arrived in Seattle, a DeafBlind woman I call "Adrijana" joined the community and a couple of years later "Lee" arrived. As I neared graduation, I grew closer with each of them, and through casual intellectual exchange they began to undermine fundamental aspects of what I had internalized in the years prior, calling into question the "need" for constant sighted intervention and expressing, on many occasions, genuine confusion about why such pervasive intervention was necessary. In 2001, I was on track to become a professional interpreter, but by the time I finished my training, I felt that my continued involvement in that capacity would cause more problems than it would solve. Still, I was fascinated by this world and felt there was much more for me to learn. So, in 2003, I left Seattle to start a program of graduate study in linguistics and anthropology. I returned on weekends and during summer and winter breaks and, in 2010, I conducted 12 months of doctoral research. I realized then that while I had been away Adrijana and Lee had turned their critical analyses into a full-scale social movement. Their premise was straightforward enough: *Vision and hearing are not necessary for life.*

In 2010, Lee and Adrijana organized a series of 20 protactile workshops for 11 DeafBlind participants in order to explore new ways of communicating and interacting through touch. I attended as a researcher, videorecording interactions and observing. I was instructed by the DeafBlind teachers leading the workshops not to interact with anyone while the group was actively involved in organized activities, and I was forbidden from acting as a source of visual information. I recorded the following in my field notes (lightly edited for typos and readability) after one of the workshop sessions:

> Each week, I bring some snacks and put them on the back table. Since the first week, I have been bringing seaweed. They come in little packages from Trader Joe's, and I find them delicious. Charlotte tried them for the first time in the second class at Lee's urging, and thought they were OK. Tonight, Eric found the seaweed. Each sheet is very thin and breakable. If you are rough with them, they crumble. He opened the package and couldn't figure out what was in there, so he felt around a little, crumbling the pieces of seaweed on the floor. Then he grabbed some of what was left in the package and put it in his mouth. Then without a tactile addressee, he walked around very dramatically, making a choking sign, saying it was disgusting! And who brought those! Yuck!!!
>
> It was really hard for me to watch and not feel responsible. The crushing and crumbling, and the mess on the floor also made me feel uncomfortable. Partially because Lee and Adrijana and I agreed that I would be responsible for keeping the room clean, but also on some deeper level—I was weighing his actions against sighted frames of appropriateness. This made me re-think all of these ways we "support" DeafBlind people. Normally a sighted person would guide each DeafBlind person to the table and explain what food was there, and the DeafBlind person might even ask the sighted person to get their food for them, so as not to knock anything over or eat something unexpected. It occurred to me that all of this "support" we provide might really be about keeping ourselves from feeling uncomfortable, not about helping them do something they couldn't do otherwise.

My perspective as a sighted person shifted as the community changed. At each moment in that process, my relationships with individuals, the profession of interpreting, and my habitual ways of engaging DeafBlind environments shifted as well. That process was not always easy. It is my hope that sighted family, friends, interpreters, and educators who work with, or encounter, DeafBlind people will read this book as one example of how your role can change and what is at stake in allowing, or encouraging, that change to take place.

Broadly construed, this book is about the relation between being in and representing the world. In representing our worlds, we achieve all sorts of aims. We fight for resources, recognition, and rights. We build consensus and articulate demands. We de-construct and re-frame. In examining the emergence of the protactile movement, this book dwells on the fact that we also struggle to exist, and there are forms of politics that operate within that struggle, day to day—not on the podium, in front of the cameras, or on social media feeds but in mundane conversations, routine ways of moving through the environment, and common-sense expectations about how the world works. Over the course of reading this book, you will encounter many reports of things that barely rise to the status of an event: a description of the way a rug is positioned in someone's house, a story about the kind of gum I chewed one day, a debate about whether a certain plant in a friend's backyard is a flower or a weed, a description of the tile in the lobby of my old apartment building, and a story about how my friend and I walked across it one day. In each case, I am trying to tease out a subtle form of politics that does not try to replace one construct with another, change dominant standards that cannot be conformed to, or break into spaces that were designed to exclude but rather to create, maintain, and protect the possibility of existence. The interactions I document rarely thematize language, identity, or other common targets of political discourse. Rather, they involve things like talking about how to get from one place to another, pointing at objects, and talking about how best to describe them. I demonstrate that these interactions, perhaps because of their apparent simplicity and concreteness, are important for understanding the stakes of the protactile social movement and, more broadly, the existential foundations of language and life.

Before continuing any further, I must emphasize that this book is not about "deafblindness," or even "DeafBlind people" in any general sense. It is a book about the inception of the protactile movement in Seattle, Washington, in a particular historical moment, and how the principles that emerged were re-interpreted by DeafBlind people in Washington, D.C., as the movement spread. In comparing these two communities, my aim is, precisely, to show that the process of becoming a protactile person is not universal but, rather, socially and historically contingent and therefore yields diverse practices, theories, and ways of being in different places and times. Only some small portion of these will be analyzed in this book and only from my perspective as a hearing, sighted anthropologist with particular relationships and experiences. This work should be read along with works by DeafBlind scholars and theorists John Lee Clark, aj granda, Najma Johnson, Sarah McMillen, Jasper Norman and Yashaira Romilus, and Jelica Nuccio among others (e.g. Clark 2015, 2017; McMillen 2015; granda and Nuccio 2018; Clark and Nuccio 2020; Johnson 2020); the growing, interdisciplinary body of research on interaction and language-use among DeafBlind people in and outside of the United States (review available in Willoughby et al. 2018); and a burgeoning body of work in anthropology on touch and proprioception in social and interactional contexts (Goodwin 2017; Goodwin and Cekaite 2018; Rutherford 2022).

1.1.1 Translation, Style, and Convention

This book contains no figures, tables, or footnotes. I chose to write this way because adding those things creates the need to provide "visual descriptions" of them, i.e. "provide acesss." In his essay, *Against Access*, John Lee Clark (2021) argues against this.

> The question I am asked most frequently by hearing and sighted people is "How can I make my [website, gallery exhibit, film, performance, concert, whatever] accessible to you?" Companies, schools, nonprofits, and state and federal agencies approach me and other DeafBlind people all the time, demanding, "How do we make it more accessible?"
>
> Such a frenzy around access is suffocating. I want to tell them, Listen, I don't care about your whatever. But the desperation on their breath holds me dumbfounded. The arrogance is astounding. Why is it always about them? Why is it about their including or not including us? Why is it never about us and whether or not we include them?

Including figures and tables would be an expedient way to create antitactile conditions, thereby putting myself in a position to provide access. It is my hope that by describing experiences, instances of language-use, and interaction in prose, I will prevent this. I try to make these descriptions clear for those who have and those who have not been in "contact space," (Granda and Nuccio 2018) or the environments that protactile people live in and give shape to together. However, if you do not understand certain things, you can skip over them for now and look for opportunities to be invited into the protactile spaces that will make them more legible.

I have excluded footnotes on esthetic grounds. Footnotes eat into the text, break up the flow, and ask the reader to digress repeatedly. This is true when the text reaches readers through visual channels, but it is especially true (I am told) when the text reaches readers through tactile channels, via Braille display. For this reason, I have minimized this convention in academic writing and the information that comes with it in order to create a pleasant reading experience. If you are the type of reader who wants more citational detail, many relevant citations can be found in the journal articles I have published in the years surrounding the publication of this book and in my dissertation.

Another potential source of confusion for people who have little exposure to protactile environments: I do not always flag the manner in which information was conveyed in a given setting. For example, Chapter 1 begins with a scene in which I am describing the setting to a DeafBlind woman.

That description was produced using ASL and received through touch. This means I was producing the description as I would for a sighted interlocutor. As I discuss below, a sighted interlocutor would have access to the visual backdrop of my face and torso, which is needed for important linguistic distinctions to be perceived. The DeafBlind receiver of my description did not have that backdrop available. Instead, their hands were placed on top of my hands, tracking their movements in empty "air space" (granda and Nuccio 2018). Tactile reception of a visual language does not make the language itself tactile. Just as English was meant to be heard, but can be partially perceived through vision (i.e. lipreading), ASL is meant to be seen, but can be partially perceived through touch. In both cases, the listener exhausts themselves trying to perceive and parse the input. It is a last resort. However, prior to the protactile movement it was the only option. If I am describing a setting in this book in which sighted people (including myself) are "providing access" to DeafBlind people, it is likely that tactile reception of ASL is the mode of communication. And again, on esthetic grounds, "tactile reception of visual American Sign Language" is an ungainly expression. My aim in sometimes omitting this information is to spare my readers an awkward and unpleasant reading experience, whether they are receiving the text via Braille or visually via print.

About names: This book is based on research that required approval from the "Institutional Review Board" at the universities where I have worked and was trained. As part of the approval process, I created consent forms that were read and discussed with every participant I write about. They consented to the process with the guarantee that I would not share their identities publicly. Therefore, I have assigned pseudonyms to participants and taken steps to obscure their identities, for example by changing the name of their home town or other information that might give away their identity. This is standard for ethnographic research and it can be considered unethical *not* to obscure the identity of participants. However, this framework is problematic, as many anthropologists before me have also noted (e.g. Weiss and McGranahan 2021). In this case, the use of pseudonyms comes with an assumption that there is a researcher who has the "theory" and the "method" and there are participants who do not. Many of my interlocutors are, like many "research participants," theorists with methods of their own. There is a line, then, that is often obscured between acting in ways that will protect "research participants," on the one hand, and failing to give credit where credit is due, on the other. John Lee Clark has also urged me (in personal communication) to think about the fact that the use of pseudonyms can work to withhold important historical information that may not be available elsewhere. In this book, I have decided that, unless I have been asked explicitly not to, I will uphold the agreement that was made in the consent process. This is, however, a temporary solution. I look forward to participating in conversations about this moving forward and plan to design consent processes to include more fine-grained options and alternatives in the future.

About "sign language": In ASL, there are many words that capture different ways of expressing the idea of "sign language" or the activity of "signing," and none of them describe what protactile people do. For this reason, protactile educators have insisted that people stop calling protactile language a "sign language" or a "tactile sign language." "Tactile language" is preferred. Along with this, using the term "signer" to refer to people who produce tactile language has also been deemed unacceptable. "Speaker," on the other hand, has been embraced by some (John Lee Clark and others) as a "higher-status" term, once reserved for spoken languages, which should be freely applied to producers of any language in any perceptual modality. For these reasons, where some might feel the term "signer" is appropriate, I use, instead, the term "speaker." To make matters more complicated, in English, and in particular in semiotic theory or theories of meaning (broadly construed), the term "sign" has a maximally inclusive meaning. Some linguistic anthropologists refer to any communicative agent who produces meaning, human or not, as a "signer" (e.g. Kockelman 2010). I am counting on the reader to be attentive to the context in which I use one term or another and adjust accordingly. It is not possible to convey my intended meanings by locking myself into one rigid association between one term and one meaning.

About translation: Unless otherwise noted, all translations are my own. In my training as an interpreter, I learned that there are different degrees of distance one can take from the message. Translating one word at a time, or providing approximations of individual, meaningful units within words (i.e. a morpheme by morpheme gloss), might be the "closest," while higher-level interpretation would take into account things like differences in background knowledge, the goals of the participants, and the projected effects of various choices in terms of how a message is packaged and conveyed. For example, in Chapter 5, I analyze several interactions where protactile linguistic expressions are used. The analysis focuses on these moments, and the details of how those expressions are produced and received are important. I therefore describe in detail *how* the message was conveyed (Section 5.4):

> ...Adrijana produced an expression foreign to ASL. Instead of extending a finger out into space along a visual trajectory, Adrijana took the DB participant's hand and turned it over so the palm was facing up. She held it in place with her left hand from

underneath. Then, with her right hand, she located herself and her interlocutor by pressing a finger into the upturned palm to mean "here." Then, she touched her finger first to her interlocutor's chest (meaning "you") and touched her own chest to mean, "me." This sequence can be glossed, "here, you, me," and the translation would be, "You and I are here."

This is an example of a relatively "close" interpretation. In uttering those expressions, the speaker could be aiming to convey a range of interactional or interpersonal meanings. At this level of interpretation, however, it is not clear what those aims are.

In Chapter 4, I quote Adrijana discussing some of the reasons DeafBlind people in her community were initially reluctant to meet with one another without interpreters present. Instead of describing in detail where her hands were moving or making contact, I describe at a higher level what I think she meant to convey:

> People already have their ways of doing things. Senior Citizens love to go to the monthly meetings [at DBSC] in order to talk to their [interpreters]! They love it because they get information from them. They don't see DeafBlind people as a source of information....

In this passage, I translated from one code to another without including any details about how Adrijana produced individual words or phrases. I also added in terms from earlier discourse that the reader would not have access to ("DBSC" and "interpreters"). This is one example of how I generated a "higher-level" interpretation. In this book, I have chosen a higher-level interpretation if my main goal is to relay what was said or how it felt to observe or participate in the interaction I describe. When I am analyzing language structure or focusing on the form of what was said, I include a layer of translation that sticks closer to the original.

Finally, a note about optimism: This book is ultimately about how Deaf-Blind people created autonomous spaces away from sighted norms and in those spaces brought an entire world into being. It is a hopeful story that I have been telling various pieces of since the completion of my dissertation in 2014. When the dissertation started circulating, I learned from several DeafBlind interlocutors that the optimistic narratives I was perpetuating had a down side. They impressed upon me the importance of recognizing grief and sadness and the fact of existential collapse. Some may read this book and feel that I am being ableist—making the process of becoming blind seem like some terrible thing, when it doesn't have to be terrible at all. After many conversations and much thought, I have come to the conclusion that under the historical and social conditions that were in place for the people I write about, becoming blind was hard. Understanding why, and how they found a way forward together, is the most important thing this book does.

1.2 This Is a Jar Containing Strawberry Jam

In the winter of 2008 on a rainy day in Seattle, I met a DeafBlind woman, Charlotte, at a coffee shop for an interview. As we found our way to a table, I described the environment. I told her about the screeching of the espresso machine and how sometimes it stopped and the room went silent. I described the subtle sound of rain and the way the windows fogged up when the cafe was full. I described the old man sitting across from us, and the white band of fine, thinning hair around the perimeter of his head. I described how people walked, how they sat, and how they ate, and I told her that there were mugs and other coffee supplies for sale up by the register. Later, when we were discussing her experiences working with interpreters, Charlotte emphasized their importance in her life (despite the many problems they also caused). She used our interaction as an example and said that without that kind of environmental information, "all I have is a conversation with you, and this coffee. I'm not really here in this place."

At that point in the history of the Seattle DeafBlind community, any sighted person, whether they were an interpreter, a friend, a colleague, a family member, or an ethnographer, probably would have found Charlotte's statement about the value she placed on interpreters unsurprising. After all, how can a DeafBlind person have a sense of where they are unless a sighted person describes it to them? Looking back on my time with Charlotte, I wonder why she and I both assumed that she needed a sighted person to take in what was around her. If she had just reached out and touched things, wouldn't she have eventually found her own tactile way of being in the cafe? What was needed, exactly, to *be* there?

For anyone who remembers or can imagine what it is like to be sighted in a cafe in Seattle on a rainy day, the description I produced might yield a sense of recognition. Your mind might skip across the surface of things, making connections I did not include. For example, the idea that fog is a sign of moisture, moisture is a sign of crowding or rain, and rain has a dampening effect on atmosphere or mood. For a person like Charlotte, who is slowly becoming blind, sequences like these will eventually fail to generate. When that happens, the limits of language will be felt.

You may wonder why Charlotte's previous experiences as a partially sighted person did not provide enough context for her to feel as if she was there with me. In order to address that question, we must ask how this kind of sequence—taking fog as a sign of moisture, moisture as a sign of rain, and so on—relates to the description I provided. How does it constitute a "context" that can render my description effective?

The relationship between language and context is a long-standing source of debate for linguists, anthropologists, and philosophers. For these scholars, the problem often begins with the indeterminate, elliptical, or fragmentary nature of "propositions," where propositions are understood as statements or "predicates" that characterize a subject or theme. For example, in the sentence, "Coats are warm," *are warm* is a predicate, which characterizes *coats*. However, in everyday contexts of language-use, you might get something more like this (Shopen 1973: 65):

Hey Mike.
What?
Ann's Coat.
O.K.

From a linguistic perspective, "Ann's coat" is functioning like an argument of a predicate but there is no predicate. This is an example of what linguist Timothy Shopen calls "functional ellipsis," which he argues is common and is easily understood by participants. The reverse can also take place, where a predicate, or phrase that asserts something about its subject, is expressed without all of its arguments. For example (Shopen 1973: 65):

Hello Henry.
What happened?
Bobby refused.
What will we do now?

Here, "Bobby refused" is missing the constituent in the sentence that would convey what it is Bobby refused to do. This is known as "constituent ellipsis," and this, too, is rampant in everyday events of language-use. In both cases, language functions as a powerful means of communication and creative expression, despite its frequent incompleteness. This fact can sometimes be accounted for via grammatical operations that involve things like "movement" or "deletion" of underlying linguistic structures (e.g. Merchant 2004) or by expanding grammatical principles beyond the sentence into larger units of discourse (e.g. Kehler 2000). However, there are cases that do not seem to draw missing propositional content from language at all, whether it is prior discourse, patterns in how discourse is constructed, or in underlying grammatical operations. Instead, the missing content is supplied by the extra-linguistic context (Shopen 1973: 66):

> Consider a jar with a label saying "Strawberry Jam." The predication is partly extra-linguistic: a predicate nominal is pasted onto its referential subject! It would create a humorous effect of overkill to have instead, "This jar contains strawberry jam."

In other words, "strawberry jam" is functioning like a constituent of the verb "contains," but the verb itself is not present. This, then, is a case of functional ellipsis, where the missing propositional content is given by the extra-linguistic context, i.e. the jar itself and its contents.

There are a couple of assumptions implicit in this analysis and the overall approach to language and context it implies. First, there is an assumption that the meaning of the jar of jam and the meaning of the label attached to it are both products of the same kind of interpretive or "semiotic" process. This is not the case. While we tend to associate the idea of "meaning" with language, the jam jar becomes meaningful in its own way as it is incorporated into an activity, such as making toast with jam. The jar can be opened, the opening accommodates a knife, and the jam inside is just the right texture for spreading. The label "Strawberry Jam," in contrast, means what it does, in part, because there is a conventional association in English between that two-word phrase and the concept of strawberry jam, which takes on additional meaning when inserted into a sentence. The jar itself and the words on the label are part of distinct semiotic processes. The jar itself does not work to characterize any theme or subject, while the label attached to it does. In other words, the "meaning" or semiotic process associated with the jar is "non-propositional," while the meaning or semiotic process associated with the label is "propositional." There is a tendency, in the analysis provided above and elsewhere, to conflate these distinct forms of semiosis. When we go about our everyday routines, walking, sitting, eating, and so on, we are not *talking* about the world, but rather *living* in it. Nevertheless, our engagements with the environment are meaningful. Understanding the difference between the kind of meaning generated by a propositional statement about the world and the kind of meaning generated by being in the world is essential for understanding the protactile movement, its consequences, and the conditions that gave rise to it.

A second and related assumption in Shopen's approach to language and context and others like it is that these two kinds of semiotic processes are interchangeable. If the jam jar weren't there, the phrase, "This jar contains…" could substitute for it and vice versa. To some extent this must be true. Entities in the world can stand in for propositional content in events of language-use. It happens so frequently, in fact, that Shopen and others who have studied elliptical speech have argued that knowing how to enact those substitutions is an important part of what it means to know a language. Propositional content can also stand in for things in the environment. If this were not the case, we would not be able to be transported into the world of a novel. However, there is a tendency for the two sides of this equation to be unequally weighted. In order to account for propositional semiosis in situated interaction (where it can appear strikingly incomplete), non-propositional semiosis is appealed to; and yet, it is not understood in its own terms, but rather, in terms of the work it would do if it were propositional. Whether or not functional equivalences like these will be effective for participants in interaction, however, depends on shared expectations among participants about how non-propositional semiosis works, and what its effects will be, such that it can be taken for granted by all involved. In other words, the approach to language in context discussed above requires us to accept that the jam jar will complete the proposition partially expressed by the label attached to it, regardless of who is involved or how their environment is structured.

These assumptions also seemed to be at play in my interaction with Charlotte, and in many interactions like it, prior to the protactile movement. From my perspective, Charlotte and I were drinking coffee and having a conversation in a place with a particular atmosphere. For Charlotte, we were just drinking coffee and having a conversation. This asymmetry meant that non-propositional semiosis could not be taken for granted. One symptom of this was that elliptical speech was ineffective. For example, imagine that upon entering, I say to Charlotte, "This OK?," meaning, "Would it be OK with you if we sat at this table?" This two-word utterance would have been difficult for Charlotte to interpret for many reasons. First, she may not know what "this" referred to. Second, without knowing what "this" referred to, the range of possible predicates would have been difficult to narrow: OK for what? Sitting at? Drinking out of? Having a conversation in?

Training to become an interpreter, I learned that these kinds of ambiguities could be avoided by adding propositional content to the interaction. This led to the production of many utterances, which, given a shared environment, would have come off as redundant or absurd. For example, standing in front of a table, I might say, "There is a table here." Waiting in line to order coffee, I might say, "We're waiting in line to order coffee." This strategy is based on the assumption that, just as propositional content can be supplemented with, or substituted for, things in the extra-linguistic context, things in the extra-linguistic context can be supplemented with, or substituted for, propositional content.

One of the main claims of this book is that when access to the extra-linguistic context is excessively constrained across a group of speakers for extended periods of time, or when that context is lacking order, the capacity of propositional content to substitute for it will slowly diminish, ultimately approaching what I am calling the *limits of language*. Beyond this limit, ordinary words and phrases will fail to elicit the expected response, or may fail to elicit any response at all, which may affect one's ability to do things like characterize states of affairs, deny that claims are true, question whether people are sincere, and suspect that things are not as they seem.

These problems tend to accrue to individuals. People living at the limits of language may appear quirky, impaired, confused, or lacking common sense. The evidence presented in this book should convince you, however, that analyzing such problems at the level of the individual, without an understanding of broader socio-historical processes and the semiotic mechanisms that facilitate them, is a mistake.

In the Seattle DeafBlind community, access to the extra-linguistic context was constrained by sighted social norms that restricted touch, not by any limitation or impairment of the individual. As a sighted person in a cafe in Seattle, there were no social norms that prevented me from taking fog as a sign. Looking across the room at the window was an appropriate and expected thing to do. Charlotte could not look across the room, but there are many signs of moisture and not all of them are visual. If Charlotte ran her hand across the window, she would encounter a lack of friction and her finger pads would slip quickly over the cold, wet surface. In order to touch the window, though, she would have to reach over a table where people were seated, and it would have been neither appropriate nor expected for her to do so in that context. She also could have gotten a sense of the atmosphere by going around the room, touching the people she encountered. She could have put her hand on their jaws to feel how quickly or slowly they were eating. She could have leaned her head in to feel the steam rise from their cups or take in the smell to see what they were having, yet none of this would have been appropriate. I explained the fog on the windows to Charlotte because from where we were sitting, given the relevant social constraints, there was no way for the concept of "fog" to co-occur with the phenomenon of fog in the speech situation, for her. I described the fog in the cafe because for me, fog is a sign of moisture, moisture is a sign of rain, and rain has a dampening effect on atmosphere or mood. I therefore had the sense that telling Charlotte about the fog would convey something about what it felt like to be there. My experience with fog and the kinds of things that can incorporate and contextualize it made my description effective *for me*. These same connections, however, could not be assumed for Charlotte.

This raises a fundamental question about language and context: How far can the world recede before descriptions of it become meaningless? Does the jam jar exist because we call it a jam jar? Does it exist because it has taken on meaning as it has been repeatedly incorporated into, and contextualized by, routine activities like making toast with jam? How do descriptions and actions, as semiotic processes, interact? Linguistic anthropologist Paul Kockelman (2006a, 2006b) offers two theoretical constructs for addressing these questions: "residence in the world" and "representations of the world." These constructs are not meant to capture some kind of "pure" or "unmediated" experience, on the one hand, and "language," "discourse," or "meaning," on the other. Nor do they imply that we cannot understand things we have not experienced "directly." In applying them here, I am claiming that there is a complex, dynamic balance that must be maintained between residence and representation, and in order to understand those dynamics, we must start from the premise that just "being here" is already a semiotic problem before any propositional content has been introduced.

1.3 Residence in the World

Residing in the world begins by cashing in on affordances in the environment for the purpose of performing actions. For humans, effectively cashing in on the *affordances* of *instruments* in our environment, such as the floor or a chair, allows us to perform certain *actions*, such as walking or sitting. In performing those actions appropriately and effectively, we take on *roles*. For example, sitting with an interlocutor in an appropriate and effective way might cast you as a romantic partner, a friend, or a business associate. Occupying such roles habitually can shape who you are, or your *identity*. These concepts, *affordances, instruments, actions, roles,* and *identities*, are for Kockelman (2006a) the constituents of the "residential whole."

Each constituent is related to the next by way of incorporation and contextualization. Affordances do not exist on their own, as abstract "features" or "properties," such as the property of "warmth," which might characterize a "coat." Rather they are aspects of the environment that are uncovered or cashed in on, as they are incorporated in and contextualized by instruments and actions. For example, if I use a fork to comb my hair (because I've gone camping and have forgotten my hair brush), the fork has been interpreted as an instrument with affordances for combing. If some other action were performed, such as eating, we would know that the affordances of the fork were interpreted differently. Actions are further incorporated in and contextualized by roles, such as "resourceful camper" or "polite eater," and roles are incorporated in and contextualized by "identities," or ways of being in the world.

When affordances are obscured, it is difficult to perform actions in socially recognizable ways, and this makes it difficult, in turn, to take on normative social roles and identities. This can lead to perceptions of "impairment," "eccentricity," and so on in the individual for whom affordances are obscured. This is an existential problem that can crop up whether or not it is identified, described, framed, re-framed, or otherwise represented.

1.3.1 Affordances

When James J. Gibson, the ecological psychologist, introduced the idea of affordances, he was concerned with all organisms (including humans) and how their environments become meaningful to them for purposes of locomotion, finding food, finding shelter, and otherwise residing in the world. For example, the surface of a lake is "walk-on-able" for a water bug, but not for a human. Likewise, chairs are only sit-on-able for an animal with knees that bend at chair height. If we had no knees, or if they were at ankle-height instead, chairs as they are generally constructed, would not be what they are. An organism going around living is interpreting affordances in their environment. However, that process of interpretation is only effective against a backdrop of organism-environment complementarity.

In Charlotte's case, we saw that complementarity was latent in the environment, but could not be presupposed in our interaction. If Charlotte had leaned up against the sighted people seated near the windows and reached her arms out over their heads, she could have encountered their crunchy Gore-Tex coats, the scratchy feeling of wool, a warm cheek, some steam rising from a coffee cup, and finally, the damp, cold feeling of the glass. The contrast between the cold of the window and the warmth of being near others may have generated a sense of being there that corresponded to my sighted sense of being there, but, due to sighted social constraints, all of this was out of reach.

In addition to the fog and the Gore-Tex, the coffee shop Charlotte and I were in was populated by particular kinds of people. I described in detail how those people interacted with their environment because I thought it would convey something about the kind of place we were in. I could have done a superficial demographic analysis based on what I could infer from appearance, or I could have counted the number of people present. These were strategies that were frequently used by sighted interpreters at the time, and in some cases, generated important information. In opting instead for a lower-level description of how people were cashing in on the affordances of their environment to perform routine actions, I was, in theory, making room for Charlotte to interpret, for herself, what kinds of people these were and, by extension, what kind of place we were in. I was trying to maximize the capacity of language to supplement the extra-linguistic context. The implicit assumption behind these efforts was that supplementation might increase indefinitely, until Charlotte was residing entirely within a description of the environment.

Around the time of my encounter with Charlotte, Adrijana and Lee were starting to push back on this and related assumptions. They argued that it is not possible to live in a description of the world, and that trying to do so will inevitably lead to the kinds of problems they observed in their community: DeafBlind people were too dependent on sighted people. There was a widespread sense of loneliness and isolation, no matter how many community events there were to go to or how many people there were around. Employment opportunities were restricted. Personal relationships were suffering. Interviewing DeafBlind people in Seattle about their lives, I learned that much of this was attributed to blindness itself, and this was due in part to the fact that becoming blind was often framed by medical professionals, such as doctors and psychologists, as an individual process involving emotions like loss, grief, and denial. As I discuss in Chapter 3, and elsewhere, becoming blind can and does lead to sadness and grief and sometimes even full-scale existential crisis. However, what was apparently never made clear to people on the precipice of that transformation was that there are non-visual ways to exist; that becoming blind is not only a loss, or reduction, of access to an objective world but also a discovery that objectivity itself is a living thing that can be created by interacting in and responding to the environment in new ways with others (Duranti 2010).

When Helen was losing the last of her vision, for example, she stopped responding to descriptions of events as if they could stand in for the events themselves. One day, her husband told her that their dog had a dead mouse and was eating it on their living room carpet. He started describing the scene. She interrupted him saying, "I'm sorry dear, but your wife is blind as a bat."

Then she crawled onto the floor, opened up the dog's mouth and smelled inside. She sniffed around the scene, and felt the dog's mouth, where there was blood. She noted that blood does not have a distinctive smell, and her curiosity was satisfied. Helen was no longer satisfied with descriptions of someone else's world. She wanted a world of her own. In the years leading up to the protactile movement, anyone could have made the choice Helen made, but once they did they would be alone. Collective norms reinforced sighted standards of appropriateness and politeness, guaranteeing that the shared world would remain at arm's length.

1.3.2 Direct Perception

The stakes of the protactile movement are captured in part by Gibson's notion of "direct perception." In introducing this phrase here, I do not mean to suggest that experience is somehow unmediated. Rather, there is, as Gibson says, a difference between "what one gets from seeing Niagra Falls" versus what one gets by "seeing a picture of it" (2015 [1977]: 139). While Gibson is focused on vision, the idea of direct perception is useful for thinking about residence and representation in any perceptual modality. Gibson explains that in a visual context:

> direct perception is the activity of getting information from the ambient array of light. I call this a process of information pickup that involves the exploratory activity of looking around, getting around, and looking at things.

This is not a denial of interpretation, mediation, or meaning. For Gibson, it is much more specifically an alternative to traditional psychological theories of visual perception that rely on "depth perception." The idea of depth perception presumes that the external world is three-dimensional, but we perceive that world visually through a two-dimensional retinal image. "Depth" is then added back into the image according to "cues."

To understand this, imagine yourself standing on the side of the road, with corn fields on both sides. The corn is high and thick. Your eye goes to the open road, the power lines on either side of it, and the place where the road meets the horizon, beyond which all of this is hidden from view. According to traditional theories of visual perception, a flat image of this scene would be imprinted on the retina. The relative size of the telephone poles growing smaller as they reach the horizon would be a "cue" that tells the mind to reconstitute the scene in three dimensions. However, Gibson argues that the third dimension is not lost in the retinal image, since it was never in the environment to begin with. We do not perceive the road that stretches out before us in terms of measurements of height, width, and depth but in terms of affordances for action. Beyond vision, for any perceptual modality, there is a lesson here: We do not live in Cartesian space. We live in a meaningful environment, which interacts with representations of all kinds but is not re-constituted in them.

From the perspective of linguistic anthropology, "direct perception" is a special kind of mediation that is non-propositional and non-inferential (Kockelman 2006a: 22). We do not infer the world: we exist within it. For the protactile movement, there is much at stake in this distinction. For example, I interviewed a DeafBlind man, Elliot, about two years after he went tactile. I asked him what had changed for him during that time. He explained that in visual environments, being blind was not something he experienced or was aware of. "It's not like I see black areas in my visual field or something," he said. "I don't see that area at all and I am not aware of it." However, he explained that when he would run into people or trip over things, he "inferred" his own blindness. He responded by taking cues and instructions from the people around him, which functioned like the "cues" of the telephone poles as they decreased in size, approaching the horizon. He was trying to re-constitute the environment in real time, as he moved through it. The problem with living that way, he said, is that your perceptual hold on reality is undermined. You don't trust yourself to interpret even the most concrete facts.

From a political perspective, an absence of direct perception across the collective meant that sighted people were the ones in a position to generate knowledge about the world, characterize the situations they encountered, and otherwise stake claims to reality. Elliot, and many others like him, just had to take their word for it. The protactile movement foregrounds the fact that even and especially at the most mundane, unremarkable level a "direct" relationship with the environment, in Gibson's sense, is a necessary basis for obtaining resources, making decisions, and building futures. If this is the case, then the first step in addressing Elliot's problems is to find a place where people are working to uncover new affordances in the environment. If, instead, Elliot tripping or falling down is interpreted as his individual problem, then the solution might be to engage in a form of politics aimed at obtaining resources to pay for interpreters or other forms of accommodation, such as assistive technologies.

Kirk, a DeafBlind man who worked for a local organization training DeafBlind people in the use of new assistive technologies, told me about a project he was working on at the time. He was testing out a GPS device that was paired with a cell phone and a Braille reader. He explained that it was a live orientation device that tells you names of streets and measurements from a present location to those streets. He said that his students had trouble using it at first—not because they couldn't understand what the device was telling them but because they couldn't understand how to apply the instructions. Many assumed that estimating the number of feet between two locations was a visual skill, and one that they had lost. Kirk said he couldn't understand why it was so hard for DeafBlind students to turn their attention to the information they could glean as their feet came in contact with the ground. In moments like these, the difference between propositions, which provide coordinates in Cartesisan space, such as "Walk 23 feet, then turn right," and the non-propositional process of interpreting affordances is foregrounded. The people attempting to use the assistive technology were not yet part of a collective effort to read affordances in the environment for routine action in corresponding ways. This meant that the instructions given by the device presupposed an extra-linguistic context that was, in effect, not there. This is what I mean by "the limits of language." Language can be used to direct attention within the world, describe, depict, and refer to the world, but it cannot substitute for it, in its entirety. In order for a language to remain operable, the world in which it operates must be meaningful to its speakers in corresponding ways, prior to any characterization of it.

1.4 Representations of the World

Representations of the world depend on residence in the world. It is also true, however, that corresponding interpretations of environments come about, in part, through conflict, negotiation, and contestation, all of which rely heavily on representational processes. Arguing about how to characterize a state of affairs, denying that a claim is true, questioning whether a sentiment is sincere, hoping for a better future, and suspecting that something is the case are all ways that interpretations of the environment can come to be aligned, dis-aligned, or otherwise related. These dynamics play out as social, political, interpersonal, psychological, linguistic, and developmental processes and have demonstrable effects on the worlds in which we reside. In other words, the relation between residence and representation is not unidirectional or static. It is dynamic and can be a crucial site for understanding the stakes of social and political action. This nexus will appear particularly important in contexts where political interventions are tied not so much to imagined communities, or constructed social realities, but to the existential conditions of those for whom social change is necessary and urgent.

Analytically, understanding how residence and representation come together requires the ability to first distinguish between them. Only then can breakdowns, correspondences, and dynamic interactions be grasped. Two characteristics that can work as diagnostics are *intentionality* and *inference* (Kockelman 2006b). Representational semiosis tends to be intentional and inferential, while residential semiosis does not. Here I am using the term "intention" in a way that diverges from ordinary English usage. Philosophers use this term to describe a range of "mental states." Intention, as in meaning to do something, is just one of many intentional mental states. Broadly, a mental state is traditionally taken to be intentional insofar as it is directed toward an object or state of affairs (Searle 1983: 1–37). Other intentional states include, for example, belief, love, elation, anxiety, irritation, and remorse (Searle 1983: 4). Intentional states correspond in many ways to "speech acts," or the things we do in speaking. Speakers can request that their interlocutor leave the room in much the same way as they can believe, fear, or hope they will leave the room (Searle 1983: 5–6). Correspondences between speech acts and mental states are established under certain conditions, for example conditions of "sincerity." If I say, "It's sunny out," I have produced an assertion (speech act), which corresponds to the belief (intentional state) that it is sunny out. If I believe it is sunny out when I assert that it is sunny out, I have satisfied the sincerity condition.

Anthropologists have shown, however, that the conditions under which speech acts and intentional states correspond are culturally and historically specific, they presuppose certain notions of personhood, and they can be more or less attenuated in different communicative contexts (e.g. Silverstein 1976; Rosaldo 1982; Duranti 1984; Ochs 1984; DuBois 1987; Hanks, 1990). For these reasons, Kockelman (2006b: 75) replaces the notion of "mental state" with "intentional status," which he defines as "a set of commitments and entitlements to signify and interpret in particular ways: normative ways of speaking and acting attendant upon being a certain sort of person—a believer that the earth is flat, a lover of dogs, one who intends to become a card shark, and so forth." Being a protactile person involves being in the world in a particular way and also subscribing to a set of commitments and entitlements to signify and interpret in particular ways.

One day in the summer of 2023, after the protactile movement had taken root and spread, I spent the afternoon with Adrijana and Sam, a hearing, sighted person who lives near Adrijana and is a frequent visitor to her home. I recorded the following in my field notes afterwards:

A couple of days ago, we were all at Adrijana's house, and Sam said, "There are beautiful white flowers all over your back yard." And Adrijana said, "They're weeds."

And Sam said, "Come on." and the three of us walked together to the back yard. We padded across the porch, which was hot, down the steps, and into the dry, cool grass. The yard was filled with white flowers. Sam and Adrijana pulled one of the flowers out of the ground, and it came with a whole complicated root system. Adrijana felt the roots and said "Weed." Sam directed Adrijana's attention to the flower—the part that had been visible to her from above. The flower was silky soft and cone-shaped. Inside, there was a delicate, yellow stamen. Adrijana felt the flower. Then she cupped Sam's jaw loosely in her palms, fingers angled out, forming a cone. She tilted the cone, with Sam's head inside, toward the sun, and said as if she were the flower, "I'm innocent."

Adrijana's argument was clear: Our eyes had led us astray. These flowers looked innocent, but their roots were taking over. In expressing her argument this way, Adrijana was not just producing a speech act, which corresponds to a mental state. She was enacting a set of commitments and entitlements to signify and interpret in a way that has arisen from, and is grounded in, a protactile way of being.

Imagine the feeling of afternoon sun on the side of your body and face. Now imagine the feeling of palms cupping your jaw and turning your face slowly toward the sun. Imagine that you feel, in that moment, like a disingenuous flower. Given this form of proprioceptive depiction (Dudis 2004), you can *feel for yourself* the truth of Adrijana's claim. At this point, you have been drawn into an intentional status consistent with a protactile way of being. It is in moments like these that residence and representation are joined. This is not a process that occurs once and for all. Residence and representation are permeated by and separated from one another, as part of routine interaction, and it is in that dynamic that the fabric of daily life coheres, threatens to come apart, or becomes a place where we struggle just to exist.

Inference is a kind of propositional reasoning. Recall that a proposition involves a subject or a theme, which is characterized by a predicate. For example, "These flowers are weeds." In this case, flowers are being characterized as a weed. Sam saw beautiful white flowers covering Adrijana's yard and told me and Adrijana about it. Adrijana contested the claim. She said that the plants Sam characterized as "flowers" were actually weeds. As I approached the plants in question, I initially thought that Sam was right because weeds are plants that people don't like. People like beautiful flowers. Therefore, these flowers are not weeds. This string of related propositions is an example of *inference*, where a proposition about an object or state of affairs leads to, and justifies, another. Adrijana also appeared to build on the assumption that weeds are plants people don't like. However, the flowers, which were the visually likable thing, were not what stood out to her. Instead, the expansive and invasive root system did. Maybe her string of propositions went something like this: Weeds are plants that people don't like. I do not like this plant because it is going to take over and kill all of my grass. This plant is therefore a weed. Sam and I both found Adrijana's characterization convincing. In the end, these two inferences—that the plants were weeds and that they were not—co-existed. Committing to one or the other, though, had implications for what kind of person each of us would be.

Recall Charlotte's statement, in 2008 just before the protactile movement started gaining ground, that without a description of a place provided by a sighted interpreter, she wouldn't really be in that place. By 2023, Adrijana had a firm grasp on her environment and when challenged she defended her position with eloquence and force. There are many transformations that had to take place between 2008 and 2023 to make this possible. Among the first of these was the emergence and spread of what John Lee Clark calls "metatactile knowledge" (2015).

1.4.1 Metatactile Knowledge

Clark explains that as a DeafBlind person who had grown up with a DeafBlind parent, he never thought to ask sighted people to describe his environment to him. It was self-evident. For others who did not grow up with DeafBlind parents, and prior to the protactile movement, that sense of self-evidence was often rigidly tied to vision. Clark recalls that every time he acted on his metatactile knowledge of the environment, people asked, "How do you know?" He wasn't always sure how to answer that question. He explains that it was "natural":

> So natural, in fact, that I didn't have a name for it, this skill that goes beyond just feeling texture, heft, shape, and temperature. I'd like to call it metatactile knowledge. It involves feeling being felt, being able to read people like open Braille books, and seeing through our hands and the antennae of and within our bodies. It involves many senses, senses that we all have but which are almost never mentioned—the axial, locomotive, kinesthetic, vestibular.... All "tactile" to some extent, but going beyond "touch."

This sense of naturalness is attributed by Clark to his having a DeafBlind parent, suggesting that early in the process of socialization he acquired the knowledge that his own axial, locomotive, kinesthetic, and vestibular responses to the environment could be treated as signs around which an intuitive grasp of the world could form. For example, knowing that when a person touches you a certain way it can be a sign of attentiveness, or when the table in a restaurant is made of particular materials it can be a sign of how expensive the meal will be. Metatactile knowledge is the knowledge that you can reach out and touch things, and in doing so you will discover a meaningful environment that anticipates your existence, offering you clues about where you can go and what you can do.

I have noticed a transformation like this in my experiences as a hearing, sighted outsider trying to understand what can count as a sign in DeafBlind spaces. For example, just as the protactile movement was starting to take shape, I returned to Seattle to work on a project at the DeafBlind Service Center (DBSC) with several DeafBlind and sighted colleagues. The following is an excerpt from my field notes, recorded during that time:

> I chew gum. Lately, it has been blueberry, orange, and tropical fruit flavors, Trident with Xilotol. I chew two pieces at a time and do not close my mouth. Janet says that since my arrival, DBSC has become very fruity. This morning, Janet and I had a meeting with Jeff and it was important. I put on some pants that were not jeans and I chose the mint gum. When I walked into Janet's office, she said she appreciated my professionalism. "What do you mean?" I said. She looked at me, a little confused, and said as if it were obvious, "The *mint*." A couple of weeks ago, Janet and I went to a DeafBlind event and political tensions were thick. She was chewing orange Trident with Xilotol, and several DeafBlind people mentioned it. DBSC seemed to be more fruity than before. Of course there were also the recent scandals.... Maybe DBSC wasn't *fruity*, exactly.

In situations like these, olfactory phenomena took on new capacities for me as potential signs of social, psychological, or political objects as they were established and negotiated around me. Mint was a sign of professionalism (obviously!) and fruitiness felt misleading, in light of the politically fraught changes taking place at DBSC.

For Charlotte, at the time I interviewed her, the potential meanings of olfactory and tactile phenomena were obscured. Even for those like Clark, the idea that touch or smell could be the basis of legitimate knowledge about the world was something that had to be protected, fought for, and insisted upon. Clark explains, for example, that when he started teaching Braille to other DeafBlind people, he was surprised to find that they didn't already understand their environment. Instead, they would ask him for descriptions not unlike those I had provided to Charlotte. Clark links this tendency to anti-tactile socialization and a desire to adhere to sighted norms of behavior. He explains:

> This is one of the things the protactile revolution is addressing, this awful way we are conditioned to yield to visual culture at our expense. As much of my tactilehood I've enjoyed, I still catch myself holding back for something as stupid as appearance—appearance within a visual context entirely outside of my reach.

Acquiring metatactile knowledge involves perceptual, psychological, and interactional processes, constrained by tensions between protactile and sighted social norms. In environments where metatactile knowledge is being generated, one person can infer the meaning and consequences of another person's behavior. "Feeling being felt" tells you something about what others are hoping for, what they think is the case, or what they really mean in saying something. It allows you to "read people like open Braille books...". In other words, metatactile knowledge is the product of non-linguistic representational processes, which are embedded in and contextualized by tactile ways of being in the world.

Since the inception of the protactile movement, a new tactile language has been emerging (Edwards 2014; Edwards and Brentari 2020, 2021). However, metatactile knowledge is treated by protactile leaders and educators as prior to, and foundational for, the acquisition of this language. In the summer of 2023, I visited a protactile training center, run by Adrijana. In the years leading up to the trip, protactile language had grown and changed so much that I could no longer follow routine conversations about things like schedules, recent events, or gossip, so I traveled to Adrijana's center for an extended stay in the hopes of getting caught up. When I arrived, I asked her for a vocabulary lesson. She told me to blindfold myself. This was a pattern. People would ask Adrijana, "How do you say...?" and she would refrain from answering and encourage them to be more attentive to the environment.

The first time Adrijana told me to put on a blindfold, I didn't know how to behave. I took hesitant little steps around the house with my arms extended straight out in front of me, worried that I would smash into a wall or trip on a step. Adrijana laughed, pushed my arms down, and said, "Zombie." She told me to pay attention to my feet, which were separated from the floor only by my thin socks. She walked around the house with me describing, in protactile language, the different textures, drawing my attention to the information those textures conveyed. She explained that you only raise your hands when your feet tell you to. Standing on the kitchen floor with me, she turned my hand so the palm was facing down. From underneath, she slid her palm across mine slowly, creating a sensation that matched the smooth feeling on the bottom of our feet. As we moved into the living room, she did the same thing, this time mimicking the feeling of carpet by making a scratching movement on my flattened, down-turned palm. As we crossed over the threshold from one room to the other, she guided my hand to the door frame, and from there to the couch, where we sat down. After repeatedly being directed by Adrijana and others in this way, I started to understand that the signs that would tell me when to raise my arms up, when to continue forward, when to turn, and when to sit down would all come through the feet.

After three weeks with Adrijana and others, I found myself perceiving my environment, attending to events, and storing memories in new and more tactile ways, which seemed readily accessible for formulating narratives in protactile interactions. One day, for example, Adrijana and I had taken a long car trip on a winding road. Later, I reflected on the trip with Oliver. It didn't even occur to me to share memories of the sunset or the swaying wheat fields. Instead, I focused on things I could feel. To describe the winding roads, I gripped Oliver's shoulders and pulled his whole torso abruptly to the right and then the left. Another time, discussing the invasive nature of blackberries, which Sam and I had just passed by on a walk, I inched my fingers up Sam's chest, as if they were vines, and slowly wrapped them around her neck. In both cases, my interlocutors responded with signs of engagement, attentiveness, and enjoyment. Adrijana refused to cede to my request for vocabulary. Instead, she insisted that I focus on metatactile knowledge. As a result, I started perceiving and remembering my environment in more tactile ways and developing a sense of what might count as a plausible or compelling representation of the world.

1.4.2 Language Emergence

Adrijana's descriptions of the floors in her home and the flowers in her back yard are organized not only by a protactile way of residing in the world but also by grammatical constraints that have emerged in the linguistic system. Prior to the protactile movement, DeafBlind people in Seattle applied strategies that have been reported in DeafBlind communities in and beyond the United States. (Collins and Petronio 1998; Mesch 2001, 2013; Quinto-Pozos, 2002; Collins 2004; Petronio and Dively 2006; Mesch et al. 2015; Checchetto et al. 2018; Iwasaki et al. 2018, Willoughby et al. 2018). Due to the fact that sign languages, such as ASL, are difficult to receive via touch (Reed et al. 1995), these strategies usually include non-linguistic mechanisms or modifications of the visual language. For example, Iwasaki et al. (2018)

describe how DeafBlind signers of Auslan manage turns at talk without the benefit of non-manual features such as eye gaze, eyebrow movements, and facial expressions that sighted Auslan signers depend on in performing corresponding communicative functions. In ASL, Quinto-Pozos (Quinto-Pozos 2002) reports an avoidance of, and restricted range of functions for, pointing signs. Petronio and Dively (Petronio and Dively 2006) report a higher frequency of the words "yes" and "no" in conversation, which they attribute to a lack of access to non-manual expressions that usually do that pragmatic work, such as head nods and eyebrow movements. In protactile communities, a more radical departure from ASL has transpired. To say that this change is motivated by sensory modality would be imprecise and uninformative since modifications of visual languages for tactile reception also involve a shift from visual to tactile channels.

The emergence of protactile language was not the result of explicit discussions about language, or "language planning." In the early 2010s protactile people were not saying, "ASL isn't working for us. Let's invent a new language." They were cultivating and exchanging metatactile knowledge as it applies broadly to interactions with people and the environment. One of the many effects of this was a radical restructuring of the language. As discussed in Edwards and Brentari (2020), ASL signs are produced with two articulators: the hands and arms of the signer. Protactile speakers, in contrast, have four potential articulators to work with: the hands and arms of Speaker 1, or the person conveying the message, and the hands and arms of Speaker 2, or the person receiving the message. The incorporation of the listener's body into the articulatory process has many consequences for the internal structure of the language, beginning with a crucial observation by granda and Nuccio (2018) that in ASL signs are produced on, and in front of, the body of the signer, or in "air space." In air space, the relative locations of signs are perceived against the backdrop of the signer's body. Receiving ASL through touch, one has access to the hand of the signer, but not the visual backdrop that is necessary for making relevant distinctions. For example, spread out your hand into a number "5." Now touch the tip of your thumb to the front of your chin. That is, roughly, the ASL word meaning "mother." Now do the same thing on your forehead. That is the ASL word meaning "father." The only difference between them is the location, and in order to distinguish one location from the other the listener needs to be able to see landmarks on the signer's face, such as the chin and the eyes, which partition the face into linguistically relevant spaces.

As I explained earlier in this chapter, in 2010, Adrijana and Lee hosted a series of 20 protactile workshops for 11 DeafBlind participants, which took place over the course of 10 weeks. The aim of the workshops was to establish new conventions for "DeafBlind to DeafBlind" communication, rather than relying on sighted interpreters to mediate. It was an experiment—no one knew exactly what the outcome would be. Videorecordings of the workshops generated 190 hours of data. In analyzing these data, a gradual shift away from what would later be called air space and toward what would later be called contact space was observed for purposes of linguistic expression (Edwards 2014). In 2015, Diane Brentari, a phonologist with special expertise in signed languages, traveled with me to Seattle and we collected a round of data which would give us a second time-point in our study of the emergence of protactile language. In Edwards and Brentari (2020), we report that protacile speakers were consistently establishing contrasts between words against the backdrop of the *listener's* body. This dramatically expanded the capacity of the "tactile modality" by tapping into previously ignored channels generated by the sense of "proprioception," as distinct from touch.

For our purposes, you can think of touch as contact with the outside of your body. Use your right hand to touch your left hand. That is touch. Proprioception, in contrast, is felt internally. For example, you are not submerged in water right now (I assume), and you don't need to see or hear to know that. You know because you can feel the position and weight of your own body in a medium (i.e. air or water). That is possible thanks to the proprioceptive sense, which includes the axial, locomotive, kinesthetic, and vestibular channels that Clark mentions in defining metatactile knowledge. The move to contact space made all of those channels available. However, it also created a problem for the linguistic system, since the articulators of at least two people had to somehow be coordinated, and efficiently enough to keep up with the demands of language-use in real time. Edwards and Brentari (2020) argue that early in the emergence of protactile phonology, the language resolved this problem by establishing conventional ways of inviting Speaker 2 to contribute to the co-articulation of signs. I am not referring to the kinds of jointly produced meanings that occur in conversation. I am talking about a lower-level kind of coordination that involves the way that the mind must work with muscles and skeletal structures to produce the forms that carry meaningful content from one person to another.

Fairly quickly, mechanisms for achieving coordination of the articulators became conventionalized (Edwards and Brentari 2020). That process involved assigning specific linguistic tasks to each of the four articulators, in the same way that the two hands in visual languages are assigned consistent and distinct tasks (Battison 1978). In order to accomplish that, new linguistic units emerged, whose sole purpose is to organize articulators for linguistic functions. These units are not found in visual languages, and their introduction into the system triggered a cascade of additional changes, including the replacement of the basic units for building words in ASL with a new set of units, and the introduction of new rules for how those units can and cannot be combined. This marked the beginning of a new linguistic system, which was no longer a piecemeal modification of ASL but rather an autonomous system rooted in proprioception and touch. This process is ongoing and a broader range of grammatical sub-systems are being incorporated as it continues (Edwards and Brentari 2021).

In order to understand the difference between tactile reception of ASL and protactile language, consider the following example. In ASL, the greeting or question "how are you" is produced by the signer alone. The hands curled into nearly closed fists come together and touch in front of the signer's torso. The wrists then rotate outward and the dominant hand completes the expression with the second-person pronoun, "you," which looks like a pointing gesture, toward the addressee. To receive this expression via touch is difficult because the small rotation of the wrists is difficult to follow and also because the pointing action of the second person pronoun is produced against the backdrop of the signer's body, which the DeafBlind person does not necessarily have access to. In PT, this same expression is derived from the action of taking someone's pulse. The speaker touches the underside of the addressee's wrist and squeezes, as if they were taking the addressee's pulse. In one fluid motion, they then touch the back of the same hand to the chest of the addressee. The second-person pronoun in PT is produced by touching the tips of the fingers to the chest of the addressee. Touching the *back* of the fingers to the chest adds a question marker to the expression. The elements of the expression, then, are: PULSE, YOU, QUESTION, and together, this has become a routine way of performing a greeting, comparable to "How are you?" in English. This expression is constrained by grammatical rules (Edwards and Brentari 2020, 2021). The fact that these rules are applied to a representation of taking a pulse is also relevant, since the activity itself is rooted in proprioception.

While the focus of this book is not the linguistic structures themselves, the problem of sensory modality is addressed as it pertains to language (e.g. McNeill 2005; Sandler 2013; Levinson and Holler 2014; Perniss et al. 2015; Quinto-Pozos and Parill 2015). Among scholars of language and gesture, the term "affordances" is sometimes used when speaking of language modality. For example, a class of verbs, such as "directional verbs" in ASL, is possible thanks to the affordances of a channel, such as the "visual-gestural" channel (Meier 2002). A type of channel, such as "visual-gestural" or "oral-aural" has affordances for a form of expression, such as "imagistic" or "analytic"

(McNeill 2005). However, these works are not aimed at analyzing the interpretation of affordances, in Gibson's sense. The concept of affordances tends to operate instead as an external motivating factor that can explain why signed languages do not conform to theories based on spoken languages. One of the broad conclusions that can be drawn from this work is that the mind of the speaker does not require any specific channel. If one channel is lacking the necessary affordances for some group of language-users, it can be substituted for another channel (e.g. Klima and Bellugi 1979). However, there is little understanding of how that process of substitution works in historical and interactional time, what conceptual tools are needed to understand it, and what significance it has for the people who carry it out.

The evidence presented in this book should convince those interested in language modality that to speak of "affordances" is to speak about language in context. To provide an account of modality and its effects on language, we must therefore understand the affordances of a given language in relation to the environment, as it is grasped by its speakers. Only in a second analytic moment can we tease apart the contributions of linguistic and non-linguistic processes and dynamics to the linguistic system itself. Read in tandem with work on the emerging structure of protactile language, the chapters that follow offer some insight into those complex dynamics and therefore into the patterns that undergird language modality and language emergence.

1.5 Life at the Limits of Language

This book is about a period of time, from the late 1970s to the early 2010s, when there were socially and politically organized efforts among DeafBlind people in Seattle, Washington, D.C., and elsewhere, to find new ways of being DeafBlind. Prior to the protactile movement, these efforts were aimed at gaining recognition from the state in order to obtain resources, which could be used to train sighted interpreters. Those sighted interpreters would then describe and depict the fading visual world in real time, as I did with Charlotte. This led to widespread substitutions, through which representations of the world were meant to stand in for residence in the world. The problems that followed from this affected the lives of DeafBlind people and those around them. Throughout this book, and particularly in Chapters 2–4, I am attentive to those effects, and what they can tell us about the delicate balance between, and interaction of, residence and representation.

For example, in Chapter 3, I analyze a videorecorded interaction between a DeafBlind man I call Roman and a sighted interpreter. The interaction took place in 2006, prior to the inception of the protactile movement. In the recording, the interpreter is describing a large and famous sculpture of a hammering man to Roman. The action is powered by some kind of motor, which moves the man's arm slowly up and down in a hammering motion. The interpreter depicts the hammering fist and its quality of movement in ASL. As a sighted person watching the recording, the description was perfectly legible, and yet, Roman seems confused by it. He holds his hand up to shield his eyes from the sun and looks around, searching for the sculpture. After a while, he gives up, and says, "I remember I saw that sculpture about ten years ago." Language, in this and many cases like it, does not and cannot substitute for the actual sculpture, and the sense of recognition one gets from memories fades over time. Walking around a city with another person taking in the sights is a way of being in a place. Just like Charlotte wanted to be in the cafe, Roman wanted to be in Seattle. In both cases, language was supposed to enable that, and yet descriptions and depictions like these often fell short, exposing the limits of language. During the historical moment this book focuses on, Roman, Charlotte, and many others were living at this limit—pushing ASL beyond its capacities to substitute for the world it represents.

Protactile leaders and theorists, rather than focusing on the capacity of language to substitute for the world, were focused on the world itself and how it could be known without dependence on vision or hearing (McMillen 2015; Clark 2017; granda and Nuccio 2018). There was a sense that if a tactile world were uncovered, language-use would become feasible again and the structure of the language would be reconfigured as needed to make that happen. Eventually, all of this did transpire, but there were obstacles along the way. This was due, in part, to the fact that restructuring the environment required representations of the environment—everything from seemingly straightforward reference to immediate objects, such as talking about the placement of chairs, to interventions in large-scale urban development projects (Chapter 6). However, while protactile language was slowly emerging, there was no viable system for generating those representations. Therefore, throughout the 2010s, DeafBlind people continued to live their lives at the limits of language.

For example, in Chapter 6, I recall an interview I conducted with Phillip, a Deaf ASL signer involved in improving access for DeafBlind people at Gallaudet University—a Deaf university in Washington, D.C. On one occasion, he explained, he was trying to solicit advice about how to resolve a problem with curb-cuts and he reached out to a few DeafBlind people he knew of. Curb-cuts are places in the sidewalk where there is a break in the curb and the sidewalk slopes down and into the street. You may have encountered the "truncated domes," or bumps, that sometimes line those sloping areas. Those bumps are there to warn blind people who are using a cane that they are leaving the sidewalk and entering the street. Where those bumps meet the smooth area surrounding them, a line is formed. That line can also be used to project a path into the crosswalk (as opposed to walking into the center of the intersection, which would be unsafe). Phillip's office had received some feedback that the curb-cuts on Gallaudet's campus were angled incorrectly. Phillip explained to me that the problem was understood. However, he said, "when we tried to get into the details of how it might be fixed, things deteriorated":

> I was signing like I always did, and [the DeafBlind person I was talking to] had his hands on me (he was completely blind). I learned later that that was called "tactile reception of visual ASL." I didn't know that at the time. So I would say something and over and over again, the person would say, "OK, but where is that?" and then they would think for a while. Then they would say, "Where am I now?" I would point this way and then that way and we would walk toward the curb in question, and then the student would say, "Where am I now?." Again, I would point and explain and again they would become confused. I knew he was intelligent and in general a very competent person. I also knew that he got around on campus on his own, so I couldn't understand what was going so wrong. I realized that the way I framed a discussion about space was flawed from the start. I thought that because he was a good student, got around on his own, he was involved in organizations, he was smart, that he could have an in-depth conversation with me about design. But I didn't realize that there was this huge gap between his experience and the way we were talking about it. Later, when I learned about protactile, it was a huge revelation.

The problem was not just one of language "modality" as that term is usually understood. The meanings of terms like "here" and "there," "this" and "that," and the sensitivity speakers must have to retrievable values in the immediate environment are all likely to break down for DeafBlind speakers (Edwards 2017; Edwards and Brentari 2021). Living with frequent breakdowns like these at "the limits of language" generates a gap between experience and the way experience is talked about.

Where the limits of language were felt, sighted and DeafBlind people alike often responded just like Phillip did. He asked what was wrong with the individual DeafBlind person. How else can you explain someone's inability to interpret such seemingly simple questions? Once Phillip learned about protactile communication, he attributed these difficulties instead to himself and his lack of protactile knowledge. In this book, I argue that when analyzed in historical perspective, it is clear that the difficulties encountered in this particular interaction could not be pinned on any individual, including Phillip. This interaction took place during a time when DeafBlind people were giving up on ASL, but no viable alternative had fully emerged. In this case, the result is a breakdown in the most fundamental function of language to direct an interlocutor's attention to objects in the speaker and the addressee's immediate environment.

In all languages, spoken and not, there is a specialized set of terms, which perform this function—they are called "deictics," which in Greek means "pointing." In English, some examples of deictics are *here*, *there*, *I*, *you*, *this*, and *that*. These expressions are used to refer to aspects of the immediate environment. In the story recalled by Phillip, there were likely two main reasons why reference failed. First, pointing signs in ASL direct attention against the visible backdrop of the signer. As was discussed above, if the addressee does not have visual access to the backdrop of the signer's body, ASL pointing signs are far more difficult to interpret. Second, as I discuss in Chapter 5, in order to refer to something it has to be there.

When Phillip's interlocutor asks, "Where am I now?" he is not asking for his longitude and latitude, whether he is facing east or west, or whether he is close, somewhat close, or far from the referent. He is asking how to relate Phillip's utterances (which are only partially interpretable) to the environmental structures in question and, more specifically, their affordances. To understand this, imagine that you are in your bed asleep. You wake up in the middle of the night thirsty. Without turning on a light, you maneuver from the bedroom to the kitchen, pour yourself a glass of water, drink it, and return to bed. On your way back, though, you get turned around. You say to yourself, "Where am I?" You feel around until you find the door knob attached to the door that leads to the bedroom. As you grasp and turn it, everything falls into place. Now imagine that instead of finding the door knob, someone is standing next to you, explaining that the door to the bedroom is "over there." In the first case, knowing where you are begins with cashing in on the affordances of the door knob. In the second case, there is only a representational prompt to do so. While these two approaches often co-occur, the latter is a poor substitute for the former.

Think about the curb-cuts and the environment surrounding them. Phillip was not really asking about the curb-cuts themselves. He was asking about how the curb-cuts might speak more effectively to DeafBlind travelers. He wanted them to say things like: *Careful, you're leaving the sidewalk and entering the road now*, or *This way to the cross walk*. But he couldn't get that far because he did not have the protactile deictic system at his disposal, nor did he understand how to interpret the world in which it was operative. The tendency, as Phillip recognizes, is to attribute those breakdowns to the cognitive capacities of the individual DeafBlind person. In Chapters 5 and 6, I argue instead that these moments are part of living at the limits of language, a condition that arose in a historical moment when a new language was beginning to emerge but was not yet fully available.

As the new protactile deictic system emerged and spread, DeafBlind people and their interlocutors could point out *this*, draw attention to *that*, and in doing so the environment took on certain contours. In a circular fashion, the linguistic system came to presuppose those contours—not only as meanings associated with linguistic forms and projected out into the world but as part of the world itself. All of this transpired in constant tension with sighted norms that dictated how people should interact with one another and their environments. In this context, each seemingly simple act of reference was simultaneously a political and existential feat, insofar as it created, reinforced, or amplified the connections between protactile ways of *being in the world* and protactile ways of *representing the world*.

1.6 Conclusion

In this chapter, I have provided the theoretical and ethnographic context needed to understand the main argument put forth in this book—that in times of crisis and collapse, people frame precipitating events, argue about causes, make their cases for recognition and resources, and otherwise represent the world in ways that will benefit them and the groups to which they belong. They also must find a way to exist. Building on a rich tradition in linguistic anthropology concerned with the many ways people make meaning, I argue that political efforts that arise in the aftermath of collapse cannot be fully understood or accounted for without careful attention to residence and representation, understood as different kinds of semiotic processes which interact with, and depend on, one another in subtle and complex ways.

2
Creating DeafBlind Identity

The inception of the Seattle DeafBlind community can be traced back to 1972 when the Seattle Lighthouse for the Blind created a DeafBlind employment program. In the decade that followed, word got out about the program in the national vocational rehabilitation system, otherwise known as "VR." VR counselors started placing DeafBlind clients in positions at the Lighthouse and the number of DeafBlind employees grew steadily. According to records compiled by former administrators at the Lighthouse and other relevant local organizations, between the years of 1980 and 1983 more than 20 DeafBlind people had moved to Seattle, and between the years of 1984 and 1987, 48 more had arrived—nearly all of them taking positions at the Lighthouse. In this and the following chapter, I argue that the primary motivation for these relocations was just having a place to be. Employment at the Lighthouse was merely a means to that end. Nevertheless, the history of the Lighthouse, its structure, and the roles it made available were critical in generating certain ways of being DeafBlind and not others.

The Seattle Lighthouse, like other organizations of its kind, combined manufacturing jobs with social services provided to the employees who were hired into those jobs (Rochester 2004). These organizations started out as "sheltered workshops for the blind," which were originally established by schools for the blind to guarantee employment for their students upon graduation. According to historian Frances Koestler (1976), sheltered workshops have played an important and contentious role in the lives of hearing blind Americans since the nineteenth century and are at the center of political discourses that have intensified since the beginning of the twentieth century. The workshops are supposed to protect blind workers from the ideological and economic fluctuations that make their employability unpredictable. For example, after World War II, blind Americans who were employable during the war were, like many other groups, suddenly and inexplicably unemployable after the war.

The stated purpose of the sheltered workshop is reliable employment for groups that are vulnerable in unstable markets. But the type of employment provided by the workshops is unusual in that workers get "dignity" and "self-esteem" instead of money in exchange for their labor (Koestler 1976: 195). The slogan, "Giving people the chance to hate Monday mornings," which can be spotted on the side of Goodwill Industries delivery trucks and elsewhere in their marketing materials, is directly related to the model of a sheltered workshop: In exchange for work, we will provide the dignity that comes with being part of the weekly rhythms of society. Monetary compensation is secondary. Those in a position to benefit from that arrangement call it "charity," but hearing blind Americans overwhelmingly see it as exploitation, and they have railed against it. More generally, they object to what sociologist Robert Scott (1969: 80–84) calls an "accommodative" approach, which focuses on creating special environments for the blind worker, instead of giving them the skills they need to find work in the mainstream. In political discourse, blind Americans claim that accommodation is actually a strategy for maintaining a large dependent pool of workers who can be exploited indefinitely, and they have advocated, instead, for an "integrative" approach.

Given these dynamics, by the early 1970s, the Seattle Lighthouse and other organizations that grew out of sheltered workshops were running low on "charity recipients." That was a significant problem for them because by then they were into multi-million dollar contracts with Boeing and the U.S. military and their workforce was opting out. According to Koestler (1976: 226), the solution was to recruit people who were blind and had other disabilities as well, since they were less of a flight risk. DeafBlind people were part of that trend and it is clear that the roles they were stepping into were problematic. However, in general, they did not respond the way hearing blind people had. They had been socialized in residential schools for the Deaf, Deaf clubs, Deaf churches, and other Deaf organizations, where "accommodation" and "integration" were reversed in terms of their political valence.

Precisely counter to blind politics, Deaf political discourse has focused on the detrimental effects of de-institutionalization, integration, and mainstreaming, since those moves often mean isolating Deaf children in spoken-language environments (e.g. Keating and Mirus 2003; Van Cleve 2007; Cheng et al. 2019). Most of the people who moved to Seattle to take jobs at the Lighthouse did so as adults who had already suffered the effects of so-called integration and had no interest in reproducing that experience. What they wanted, by the time they got to Seattle, was a place where they could be DeafBlind. Fair compensation and opportunities for advancement were not their main concern.

For example, Adrijana ended up in Seattle in her 30s after spending much of her deaf (partially) sighted childhood in hearing environments alone. After a short period of time in a Deaf school, she was transferred to an "oral" program where spoken language was the only permitted means of communication, and from there she went on to a hearing high school without interpreters. When she described the isolation and loneliness of that experience, her eyes filled with tears. She said: "When I graduated from high school, I found out that my peers had made up a name for me. Apparently, no one knew my name and they didn't bother to ask. When I walked across the stage at graduation, they announced their made-up name instead of my real name." She shook her head, and said, "I spent four years with those people, and they never even knew my name."

Growing up, Adrijana had been punished, sometimes physically, for trying to communicate with gestures or signs. Years of her education had been wasted doing little other than slowly pronouncing individual English words. It wasn't until she went to a Deaf college that she had the opportunity to be a part of a social world. The ASL she learned as a child came back slowly and after some time, she found herself immersed in a vibrant social setting. She met the man she would marry, found a field she wanted to pursue, and felt that finally her life was on track. Not long after, though, her vision deteriorated and Deaf environments started to feel as unwelcoming as the hearing environments she had grown up in. By the late 1980s, she was having difficulty with her job and her relationships. She could tell that the life she had was not going to be feasible for much longer, but she also knew about Seattle, and she was optimistic that if she went there it would be like college had been before—a place where communication and interaction would, once again, feel natural. With this in mind, she found a job in Seattle and relocated. For Adrijana and many others, the particulars of the job weren't that important. She needed a place where she could be DeafBlind, and to her, that was inextricably tied to communication.

Others described communication access as a main reason for moving to Seattle as well. For example, Rebecca moved to Seattle from Nevada in 1985. She had grown up around sighted Deaf people, but she said that as she lost her vision, she became isolated:

> For a long time, I lived with my mom. I didn't work, because it was really hard to find a job. I had to rely on SSI [Supplemental Security Income] and stay with my mom, and my two sisters.

"Everyone would go to work," she said, "and I would stay at home alone and watch TV." When I asked her if she ever went out with friends or spent time with people outside of her family she said, "Unfortunately, many people my age kept disappearing. I had one good friend who was a teacher." About her decision to move to Seattle, she said that the job at the Lighthouse was not what she had envisioned for herself, but:

> the DeafBlind community [in Seattle] was growing at that time, which was great, and DBSC was just being established. At DBSC, I learned about SSPs ["Support Service Providers"] who could help me with reading my mail, going to the store, etc. The DeafBlind community here was fantastic. It was so much better than Nevada. There was a DeafBlind community in Nevada, but it disappeared. So I decided to try and settle here in Seattle, and work for the Lighthouse. I realized there was a better life for me here.

Rebecca's reasons for moving to Seattle were related to having a place to be, populated by things and people, which gave her something (anything!) to do. It wasn't as if she was going from one life to another. Life itself was eroding (the people and the community were "disappearing") and against that backdrop, Seattle appeared as a life raft. The job itself was a concession. In recalling her work history at the Lighthouse, she told me that one of her first placements was in a department that manufactured fire fighting equipment. She said:

> They sewed sleeping bags for firemen, but it wasn't something I was good at. I tried, but it was frustrating. They noticed that I wasn't very fast at it, so I started assembling mops, and then also canteens. I went back and forth between several departments. But after a while, the department making the sleeping bags closed down because they weren't making enough money on it. So I started doing work on the Boeing contract—mostly filing. But I used to get really sleepy doing that job. It was incredibly boring.

Still, Rebecca was glad she had the job because she could live in Seattle, where special services made it possible to carry out tasks like grocery shopping and attending community meetings and events. At home in Nevada, she would be sitting at home alone instead. Her main concern was being in an environment that enabled communication and interaction. Fair compensation, intellectual stimulation, and other factors were less important.

With communication access came intelligibility, as well. Rebecca and many others who moved to Seattle from elsewhere said that the mode of access they chose made them legible as a particular kind of DeafBlind person. People who communicated by touching the hands of the ASL signer were "tactile people."

People who chose instead to stand far away from the ASL signer, were "tunnel-vision people." No one in Seattle thought that you were backing up because you were aloof, or you were touching them because you were interested in them romantically.

However, intelligibility was made possible by the fact that DeafBlind people were communicating in idiosyncratic ways, across different modalities, and that caused problems of its own. The Lighthouse staff recognized this early on as the DeafBlind employment program started to grow. Communication between employees was so strained, in fact, that physical fights were not uncommon. I interviewed Joey, who was one of the people called in to address the problem. He was Deaf and his official title was "Communication Specialist." He explained that at that time, the DeafBlind employees "had really mixed backgrounds. Some of them had limited exposure to language in general because they had not had access to a perceptible language in the years when first language acquisition usually occurs, or they used a different sign system, such as 'Signed Exact English,' which is an invented system that attempts to represent English, manually. It was just like deaf people who were not blind," he said:

> Many came from hearing families, so they had really weak foundations in their language development. When DeafBlind people communicated directly with one another there were all kinds of misunderstandings that would lead to accusations and fighting. So as a communication specialist, I would have to intervene and explain, "that person can't see you. They have to use tactile reception, so you have to sign tactually to them." Or maybe one person doesn't really know English and the other one is throwing big [fingerspelled] English words at them and they start calling each other names.

The individuals who were all lumped together at the Lighthouse would have been part of very different networks in larger Deaf communities and even if they were sighted Deaf people they might have had some trouble communicating. These problems were never sorted out because sighted intervention became so ubiquitous that DeafBlind people rarely had to communicate directly with one another at all. Instead, they communicated through sighted interpreters. This was possible, in part, because Seattle Central Community College started producing sighted interpreters trained specifically to work with DeafBlind people, and the number of qualified interpreters grew rapidly.

2.1 Building a Bridge

Seattle Central Community College established a program for Deaf students in the 1960s and an interpreter training program in the 1970s. According to Laura, a Deaf student who was there in the late 1970s, there were about 100 Deaf students enrolled at the time. Some took two years of general requirements and then transferred to a four-year university, such as Gallaudet. Some learned technical skills like boat-building or mechanics. The Deaf program and the interpreter training program were housed in the same building so there was a lot of interaction between hearing and Deaf students. Laura said:

> It became really common for people to get together in the cafeteria, and no one cared if you were Deaf or hearing, as long as you were signing. It was a really thriving social scene. That's what it was like back then.

Early on, when DeafBlind people moved to Seattle to work at the Lighthouse, they were part of a very small group. Given the diversity in linguistic, cultural, and educational background, it was likely that they would either not be able to communicate with other DeafBlind people or that they would have nothing at all in common with them and would not feel compelled to communicate with them. Seattle Central Community College was an important resource for broadening the pool from which potential interlocutors, friends, and communication supports could be found, and they were also seen as a bridge to the "hearing world." Early on, ties between the Lighthouse and Seattle Central were informal, but over time, the relationship was embedded in institutional structures.

First, a small number of specialists with ASL-related expertise who were affiliated with Seattle Central in some capacity, were hired at the Lighthouse in permanent positions. In 2010, I interviewed Dawn, who was one of those specialists. She explained that the institutional culture of the Lighthouse at the time was very different from what they, as interpreters (who were almost exclusively women), were used to and they did not encounter a warm welcome upon arrival. In Dawn's words:

> We were relegated to a corner and given one tiny desk to share between four people. "four pairs of knees all trying to share the same knee-hole" [laughs]. Then Mary brought in a tiny sewing desk for me, and I thought, "That's fine, I don't need much. I'm going to be out doing stuff anyway." We were told to stay out of the front area [where serious business was taking place].

However, according to Dawn, their team was young and energetic, and almost immediately they started to win over the "stuffy manufacturing executives":

> You know, you run into the president's office, and say, "I need your car keys", and he says, "My car keys?" and you say, "Yeah." And he asks you why, while throwing them your way, and you say you'll tell him later. We were this flash of life in an otherwise dimly lit room.

Dawn suggested that within the walls of the Lighthouse, the 1950s were alive and well—"drinking lunches" and all. She and the others who came in with the DeafBlind program brought the '80s with them:

> It was like that. But you know, they were trying to find common ground. We [the staff of the DeafBlind program] have always stuck out like sore thumbs. It's like Mary Poppins descending into stuffy George's house. This is really a very conservative manufacturing company, and we have always been something else.

In these early years, there was a sense more generally that the Seattle DeafBlind community was adjacent to local institutions—drawing resources, but not being defined or subsumed by their structure.

At the Lighthouse, adjacency had to do with the fact that organizations of its kind traditionally employed or served hearing blind people. Communication specialists and interpreters who came to work at the Lighthouse in the 1980s had been educated in programs that focused on the history, culture, and language of Deaf people and the analytic skills needed to mediate between their minority perspective and that of the larger and more dominant hearing society. When they came to the Lighthouse, they had to learn how to extend their knowledge and expertise to include things that would be relevant for Deaf people who were also blind or becoming blind. Some things required improvisation, while others fit fairly neatly into the structures, categories, and practices that were already in place in this new institutional environment. For example, one of the sighted specialists was hired to teach "independent living skills," a recognizable category in institutions that serve blind people. These classes included instruction on how to cook without vision, how to read Braille, how to label one's clothes with Braille labels to keep track of the colors, and so on. The Department of Services for the Blind (DSB) provided these services, but only in spoken English, since nearly all of their clients were hearing.

When the numbers of DeafBlind people started growing in Seattle, it became cheaper and more effective to train people who already knew ASL to provide the training directly rather than hiring interpreters. At DSB, these techniques or strategies were taught, for the most part, by sighted experts to adults who had become blind. Given this distribution of expertise, tactile reception of ASL fit in easily as an additional "strategy," or "tool." Just as Braille was a tool that helped people access written English, tactile reception of language was treated as a tool that could help people access ASL. Fitting DeafBlind reality into the categories and authority structure of the Lighthouse, then, was one factor that contributed to the maintenance of visual modes of communication and prevented DeafBlind people from building intuitions about tactile environments.

Meanwhile, interpreting and translation, framed explicitly as bridge-building, actually reinforced these anti-tactile tendencies. Interpreters are trained to mediate between languages—in this case ASL and English—at the level of pragmatic inference. The goal is to capture not what the speaker says, but what they mean to *convey* in a way that will be interpreted as grammatical and culturally appropriate to the addressee. If this is the starting place and the addressee is blind, the most reasonable thing to do is "add in" the information needed to draw the relevant inferences. For DeafBlind people, this meant that more and more of the environment was described, and less and less was lived in. At the time, moving in this direction was viewed as a reprieve from encroaching blindness. It was not a bridge between tactile and visual worlds, but a bridge leading back to the world they once knew. If a person had stopped going to church, or attending dinner parties, for example, they could now return to those activities, with an interpreter. If they had stopped attending group meetings at work, they could now do so with an interpreter. If they had stopped going out past dark, they could now do so with an interpreter. The world, as it was already known, could be preserved or prolonged.

In the absence of a tactile world and tactile language, interpreters were also necessary for political organization. With their involvement, the Seattle DeafBlind community achieved political recognition from state government, which led, in turn, to the creation of the DBSC—an institution that would play a crucial role in the community's future.

2.2 "We Need Interpreters"

When I asked people about the origins of DBSC, the response often began, "Do you know Dan Mansfield?" And then the following sequence of events was recounted: It was the late 1980s. Every year, there was a new influx of DeafBlind people, and as the community grew, flaws in the local infrastructure became more obvious. Resources were taxed and something had to be done. To convince decision-makers of this need, the community turned to Dan Mansfield—a DeafBlind man, known for his good looks and his charm. His aim would be to convince representatives of the Washington State government that there was a real and pressing need for interpreters, and that those interpreters had to be provided by a new and independent DeafBlind organization.

I pieced together this part of the community's history digging through big boxes of old documents and newspapers. Some of it came from the Lighthouse archives and a lot of it came from ethnographic interviews. On the points I have just outlined, there was significant convergence across interviewees, but the following story was almost exactly the same every time:

> Looking fantastic, Dan walked confidently toward the committee. They were seated at a long table on a raised platform at the front of the room. Dan told the interpreter, who had accompanied him, not to speak, and then took his place before the committee. He pulled a stack of index cards out of his pocket. Each card had a printed letter on it. He began to spell his message one letter at a time: "I. A. M. . . ." And then he slipped and all of the cards fell on the floor. People jumped up and tried to help him collect the cards, and it was awkward and uncomfortable for everyone. Finally, he stood up and started again with the cards. This time, though, they were out of order and his message was indecipherable. There was no way to interrupt him because the interpreter had been instructed not to participate, so he went on like that, slowly spelling unintelligible words. Then he told the interpreter to start interpreting for him again. All he said to the committee was, "We need interpreters." And DBSC has been funded ever since.

As I inquired further about the history of DBSC, I learned, of course, that there were broader efforts, undertaken by many, to achieve political recognition and to secure funds for services.

One such effort was led by administrators at the Lighthouse. Working with DeafBlind members of the community, they created a "needs assessment" and shared it with the directors of all of the relevant state agencies. Leah, one of the Lighthouse administrators in charge of the project, explained in an interview:

> One of the key things we did was put together a matrix. It was done by hand because it was before computers. It was a grid sheet. We had services and organizations, one on each axis, and we put an X where there were services, and no X where there were no services. That became a tool for us to make our case.

During a 12-month period of dissertation fieldwork, I found the original matrix in a box of pictures and old newsletters at the Lighthouse. It was hand-drawn and the ink had faded. Following up on the stories I had heard about it, I interviewed Al, who was the director of DSB at the time. He told me:

> By the time I saw the needs assessment, [Seattle] was a place of choice for Deaf-Blind people. Large numbers, proportionately, so it created a real challenge for metro, [VR, DSB, and other state agencies]. We had a real problem.

The solution, he explained, was to create DBSC—a separate non-profit organization that would provide the services other agencies couldn't. One of the key things DBSC needed to do was secure funds for specialized interpreters who could act as guides, relay environmental information, and provide transportation outside of work hours. A more permanent, institutional structure would, as Al said, ensure that DBSC "was not subject to the whims of whoever happened to be directing the three agencies."

According to Leah, everyone thought it was a great idea, but no one was jumping out of their seat to pay for it. So the aim at this point was to convince the governor's office to establish a bill that would secure funds for DBSC. In order to achieve their goal, political representatives had to become aware of the need for specialized interpreters. Groups of DeafBlind people and sighted advocates and interpreters started making regular trips to talk to individual senators and representatives at the capitol with the goal of demonstrating, in person, the important role interpreters played. One sighted interpreter had a Volkswagen bus that everyone would pile into and go down to the Capitol for the day. They planned their appearances strategically, showing up, for example, during the lunch hour on days when important meetings were happening. There were sleepovers the night before, where people would practice their speeches repeatedly, until they were concise and flawless. Real relationships were growing and sighted interpreters, according to both DeafBlind and sighted people, were abundant and able to volunteer their time.

In addition to demonstrating the need for interpreters, activists also wanted the legislature to force the relevant state agencies to put a proviso in the budget to secure funds for interpreters, regardless of who happened to be the director of the obligated agency. During this time, DeafBlind people were a persistent presence on the Capitol campus. For example, Al told me about a particularly memorable moment when he felt political recognition had been achieved:

> Jim McDermot was chairman of the Ways and Means committee. It was really hard to get a meeting with him, and I remember the DeafBlind folks were down that day.

> We had come to his building—his office was in a suite. There was a waiting room and a conference room. And he had an office in the back in the ground floor of this building. Dan Mansfield and four or five people were standing in the hallway outside of his door. He was leaving his office, about to go out to the capitol. He was so hard to meet with, that typically people would ambush him—*Senator can I walk with you*. Every once in a while, he would see someone he wanted to talk to, and he would walk with them, but most of the time, [he would bolt]. So he stepped out and he glanced down the hall, and he saw several DeafBlind people talking to each other and the interpreters. And he stopped and stared for about a minute watching their communication. I observed this, and I thought, "Holy hell. He never exposes himself to everyone like that." And I thought, "They got him. He is seeing what the challenge of communication is—in one respect anyway—and they've got his attention."

According to Al, this kind of fascination played a significant role in the DeafBlind community's political success. In a representative democracy, no one should care about this tiny group of people and what they are asking for, at least in theory. But Al said that for this senator, and for others, there was a "lost tribe" aspect to it:

> Here's this thing that you didn't know exists, and it exists. And DeafBlind people were saying they wanted to come into the fold. They weren't trying to impress upon us their particularity or their specialness. They just wanted what everyone else wanted.

Political recognition led to increased resources, which drew even more Deaf-Blind people to Seattle. DBSC had a dependable annual operating budget. Work and personal lives could therefore be separated since interpreting services were provided outside of the Lighthouse. There were also advocacy services provided and space for community functions that were not associated with work. All of this was made possible by an elaborate network of highly specialized interpreters that had been built in the years prior, and it was largely about securing resources that would pay for those interpreters.

From the earliest years of the Seattle DeafBlind community, sighted mediators have played an instrumental role in communication. For example, several people I interviewed told me about a Halloween party, which was held in apartments owned by the Lighthouse. A small group of Deaf, DeafBlind, and hearing people attended the party. ASL was the language everyone had in common and people just "did what came naturally" to communicate. There were no official interpreters working and at least some of the sighted people present thought about guiding and relaying information about the environment as part of "hosting." One person explained: "If someone looked lost, someone else would help them find what or who they were looking for." Since blindness was so stigmatized elsewhere, a willingness to do simple things like this was unusual. It was also very different from what some of the DeafBlind people had anticipated for their futures. For example, some were told that once they went blind, they would only be able to spell words out letter by letter using the manual alphabet, while others couldn't imagine any life at all without vision. So, as one sighted participant explained, "There was a lot of excitement. What had been impossible was suddenly possible, and everyone was really excited about it." With the establishment of DBSC, its interaction with the interpreter training program at Seattle Central Community College, and the employment and community programs at the Lighthouse, early methods for addressing communication like these were ramped up and reinforced by institutional structure.

2.3 DeafBlind Identity

As modes of communication became conventionalized, ways of being Deaf-Blind emerged which were not rooted in the world, but in conventions for working with sighted interpreters, through whom DeafBlind people *accessed* the world. By the 1990s when I entered the community as an undergraduate interpreting student, "tunnel vision" and "tactile"—terms that derived from two approaches to access—came to represent the main identities a DeafBlind person could assume. In both cases, the aim was to maintain connections to the world of the sighted. In order to prop that system up, the extensive sociopolitical efforts I have just recounted, were required.

In 2006, just before protactile practices began to emerge, I asked Adrijana what the word "community" in "DeafBlind community" meant. She said:

> The only basis for community is an external influence, against which a group of people needs to protect themselves. Otherwise, what's the purpose of a community? Communities are for building internal strength in order to protect yourself and other people who are in a similar position. It is a place to feel safe, but against who? If there is no answer to that question, then why bother? For us, it's obvious. Hearing people make all kinds of unnecessary barriers for us that we have to find a way around. There are social issues and economic issues. On every level we have things we have to fight for. So even though we have nothing in common with each other, and we may not even like each other on a personal level, we have to work

together to try to improve what we have and what we can do. We need each other. We're not really a community based on a common language. There is everything from ASL, to people who were never really exposed to language, to people who grew up hearing, speaking English. Likewise, we're not really a community based on common life experience. We all come from very different backgrounds. Still we are bound to each other in certain ways.

For Adrijana, the Seattle DeafBlind community was an internally diverse group, not tied together by a common language, or even by common communication practices. The "community" was a political alliance, aimed at pushing back against dominant norms that generated unnecessary barriers. This statement, while particularly clear and elaborated, was similar to things I had heard when I was in training to become an interpreter. My teachers and professional interpreters in a mentoring role would say, "DeafBlind people are all different. One approach will not work with them all," or "Communication in the DeafBlind community is very diverse." Later, during my time serving on the board of several Deaf and DeafBlind non-profits, the same warnings were issued: "Remember, not everyone comes from a 'Deaf culture' background. We have to serve everyone." DeafBlind identity in the Seattle DeafBlind community was established as an oppositional category, used to obtain resources from local and state government to pay sighted interpreters, and other professionals, such as advocates, which required institutional resources, such as physical space, and funding to pay professionals, train them, and coordinate their services with the needs of community members.

There were significant benefits to having an institutional structure that could provide services in a consistent and sustainable way (very few places in the United States had such things). However, problems persisted and over time worsened. By the time I started my dissertation fieldwork in 2010, a new protactile theory was beginning to be articulated by DeafBlind leaders to explain the problems they had and also to map out a new course of action. From that perspective, in retrospect, establishing a DeafBlind identity was critical. The protactile movement would have never emerged if it weren't for the availability of physical spaces where meetings and workshops could take place, bus drivers who had been trained to guide DeafBlind people onto buses, sighted people who could mediate service encounters to make grocery shopping, banking, attending community events, and other necessary activities possible. At the same time, there was a sense that "community" had been built on an unstable foundation. In the next chapter, I trace the effects of this on the collective—its practices and its politics—as well as on individuals, as they took on the DeafBlind identities available to them at the time.

3
The Collapse of the World

As members of the Seattle DeafBlind community became blind, the visual worlds they once knew buckled and eventually collapsed. Individual and collective attempts to re-build followed, some of which were deemed more successful than others. This chapter analyzes those attempts in order to understand how worlds collapse, how signs of collapse are detected, and what kinds of interventions are possible. As I discuss in Chapter 1, Paul Kockelman (2006a: 22) breaks the world, or what he calls "the residential whole," into five constituents: affordances, instruments, actions, roles, and identities. The constituents are related to one another by way of incorporation and contextualization. When the world is up and running, it contains instruments, which are grasped in terms of their affordances for performing actions. In performing actions routinely, a role is taken on, and in regularly taking on roles, one has an identity:

$$\text{affordance} \rightarrow \text{instrument} \rightarrow \text{action} \rightarrow \text{role} \rightarrow \text{identity}.$$

Identities contextualize and incorporate roles, roles contextualize and incorporate actions, actions contextualize and incorporate instruments, and instruments contextualize and incorporate affordances. Breakdown anywhere along that line is part of life, but collapse occurs when the relations between the constituents break down in such a way that you can no longer be who you are.

Collapse is always the culmination of some larger historical process, but, for the individual, there will be a discrete moment when the signs of collapse can no longer be ignored; when all of the equipment has broken down and there is nothing left to work with; when action feels terminally restricted, and you realize that existence itself is at stake. In a time of collapse, that moment of realization will repeat itself, and between repetitions there will be periods in which fantasies of ordinary life proliferate. You pretend that the world is still intact, and you recruit others to your fantasy. When pretending is no longer possible, there are sober or frantic attempts to put things back together. In this chapter, I analyze that process as it unfolds over the course of about 30 years of Seattle's DeafBlind history. I argue that exiting cycles of collapse depend on the order in which the constituents of the residential whole are re-assembled. Starting with identities (the thing that depends on everything else), rather than affordances (the thing that everything depends on), will likely lead to subsequent cycles of collapse.

The people in this chapter were all actively involved in Deaf networks, organizations, and communities across the United States and had firmly established lives as sighted or partially sighted Deaf people before relocating to Seattle. At some point they were told that they would become blind. For many of them, this information was delivered in a crude way by medical professionals with no accompanying instructions for how to live as a blind person. The worlds they resided in at the time offered many roles and identities, but all of them required the ability to adhere to sighted norms and standards. When they were told they would be blind, they couldn't imagine how life would go on at all. The problem was particularly acute for those who were informed of their impending blindness before the time of the internet and before interpreters in medical settings were a legally protected right.

Glen, for example, grew up in the Midwest. His family had a farm, which he and his siblings visited on weekends and over holiday breaks. Otherwise, he lived at the residential school for the Deaf. Although he noticed early on in his childhood that he had a harder time than other kids playing sports and communicating in the dark, he didn't think it had anything to do with his eyes. It wasn't until he was in his 20s, when he was driving at night and got into an accident, that he started to suspect he "might need glasses." He visited an eye doctor and underwent an exam, but he did not receive glasses. Instead, he was referred to the Department of Services for the Blind, or "DSB." This was prior to the Americans with Disabilities Act, which meant that there were no sign language interpreters and communication with the doctor was limited. Glen's understanding was that DSB would be better equipped to provide glasses than the doctor he had already seen, and yet, an uneasy feeling set in. The following is his account of what happened next:

> I drove to DSB and parked my car far from the entrance so no one would think it was strange that I was driving. I went in and found Ann. My appointment was at 1:00. Ann came out and met me, pulling me by my forearm into her office. I thought, "what is this lady doing?" But she just went right on, smiling, and pulling me into her office. Finally, we sat down in her office. She brought out a Braille book, and some math cards. I had no idea what was going on. I couldn't imagine why she was giving me all of this stuff for blind people. I wrote on a piece of paper that she must

have misunderstood or something, that I only came to get glasses. I told her I had perfectly good vision. She wrote back: "You're going to be blind in 15–20 years."

This was a common experience for the DeafBlind people I interviewed, particularly in the 1970s and 1980s. After a series of confusing encounters with hearing medical professionals, a crude message was scrawled on a piece of paper. Glen was also not unusual in his response. He pretended like the whole thing had never happened. His reason was straightforward. He said:

I felt that [if people found out], I would lose all of my freedom. I wouldn't be able to drive, or go anywhere. I would just have to sit some place all day long, bored. I assumed there was nothing but an empty existence for blind people.

In that moment, Glen was forecasting what I call collapse. Once he lost his vision, he felt that he would have no role and no identity and he attributed this to the fact that action would be terminally restricted. He would "just have to sit some place all day long." His analysis was linked explicitly to the equipment woven into daily life in his region. Glen lived in a place where people drive to get where they are going. Without a car, it would be impossible for him to do anything, and therefore be anyone. Affordances in the environment that might have enabled travel (and therefore action), without the use of vision, remained hidden in that place and time in Glen's life.

Adrijana, who had also moved to Seattle from elsewhere, told me a similar story. She had just graduated with a degree in biology and was doing research she loved when her vision deteriorated and her life as a biologist fell apart. When I asked her why she couldn't find another way to pursue her work, she said there was no way around the microscope. In general, whether it was cars or microscopes or some other instrument, that was how people read the signs of impending collapse: The equipment breaks down, and not just in ways that make life inconvenient. It breaks down in ways that make it impossible to continue being who you are.

However, there is another way to interpret those experiences. One could assume that the equipment isn't the problem. The point is that people need to embrace a DeafBlind identity before they can move on. That was the way the Seattle DeafBlind community went in the 1970s and 1980s—they started with *identity*. Identity was such a hurdle that Glen and many others like him spent years in a holding pattern, disclosing their diagnosis to a select few, or no one at all. They went on with their lives as if nothing had happened, but as their vision deteriorated strategic compensation was required. They learned to linger in the back of the room where their tunnel vision would capture a wider swatch of activity. In conversations, they stood far away from the person they were talking to so they could see more of them. When that became impossible, they honed their skills of inference, and when that failed, they pretended to understand, drove as if they could see, and imagined that the people they were talking to were listening. Eventually, they limited themselves to one-on-one conversation. Slowly, their range of activity narrowed. They no longer stayed out past dark or went to parties. They didn't meet friends in restaurants or bars with low lighting. They stopped driving and eventually they stopped taking public transit too. If that process continued for an extended period of time, people became withdrawn and isolated. It is easy, when you've been alone for too long, to forget how to behave in recognizable ways. When you finally do re-enter society, your strange behavior can drive people away. That cycle of isolation, gone unchecked, can hollow out a life.

In interviews, DeafBlind people who had since moved to Seattle recalled the end of their lives in the places they came from. They described spending weeks on end doing nothing; being worried about how they would get food; how they would know when their baby was crying; how they would pay their bills. They talked about how ordinary objects hid themselves, and how eventually all of the people disappeared too. They associated those experiences with the demise of what they would later would refer to as the "old world," the "Deaf world," or the "visual world."

Then, in the mid-1980s, something hopeful started to happen in Seattle and word got out. As I noted in Chapter 2, 48 DeafBlind people moved to Seattle between the years of 1984 and 1987. Those who were part of that influx reported a sense of relief, and in some cases elation, when they arrived. They had accepted that they were DeafBlind and had moved to Seattle. Through interpreters, guides, and other specialized professionals, action of all kinds was restored.

Seattle was a place where crucial services were available and for many, it became a badly needed alternative to existential crisis. However, certain vulnerabilities were built in as the community grew. Recall that the constituents of the residential whole contextualize and incorporate one another. There are dependencies between them and those dependencies are not bi-directional. Identity is the thing that depends on everything else and everything else depends on affordances:

affordance → instrument → action → role → identity.

For the first thirty years of Seattle's DeafBlind history (from the 1970s to the beginning of the 2000s), the reconstruction of the residential whole began with identity, not with affordances. The procedure was as follows: A person accepts that they are DeafBlind (identity), which reinstates their capacity to be a professional, a friend, or a community member (role). This, in turn, makes it possible for them to go about their business in the world (action). However, as we will discover in what follows, those benefits were temporary and led ultimately to subsequent cycles of collapse. My claim is that this approach failed because things were proceeding backward through the constituents of the residential whole.

In what follows, I draw on interviews and ethnographic observations to elaborate on each of the stages in that process. First (as we have already learned), the equipment breaks down—not just in ways that are inconvenient, but in ways that make it impossible to be who you are. To cope with the situation, you find yourself taking on an identity, which will make accommodations available to you (Section 3.1). However, "accommodation" tends to reinforce what is appropriate for *them*, not what is effective for *you* (Section 3.2). As that situation wears on, there are signs of "strain": You are doing things that are appropriate but not effective, effective but not appropriate, or neither appropriate nor effective (Kockelman 2006a: 39). Strain is a part of life, but when you find yourself adhering to someone else's standards and norms to such an extent that effective action is foreclosed entirely for you, the ordinary struggles of life can give way to *existential strain* (Section 3.3). This is where the signs of collapse become impossible to ignore.

Under the weight of existential strain, it is impossible to commit, or to internalize, and therefore be able to anticipate, the meaning or effect of your actions (Kockelman 2006a: 61). Commitment is inherently problematic, but when it is rendered impossible; when misconstrual of your actions is all there is; when your intentions are, as a rule, twisted, diverted, or replaced, this is a serious warning sign: The world you are in is teetering on the brink of collapse (Section 3.4). At some point you find that in place of your former life, you now spend most of your time trying to keep things life-like. You throw up a replica or sketch a memory in your mind, but as time passes, your experiences begin to feel like types or examples of experiences. Lacking stimulation, your thoughts drift over the past so many times that your memories lose their structure and texture and begin to feel homogeneous or blank (Section 3.5).

Understanding this process helps contextualize the protactile movement (Chapter 4) and the language it is giving rise to (Edwards and Brentari 2020). The framework developed in this chapter should also be relevant for anyone anywhere who has ever wondered, or is currently wondering: *Is this the beginning of the end*? If you are one of those people, this chapter might make you nervous, but it should also offer hope. It is true that when the constituents of the residential whole are re-assembled in the wrong order, collapse ensues. However, when they are re-assembled in the required order (affordance-first!), undiscovered worlds are revealed, and new modes of existence become possible.

3.1 Embracing DeafBlind Identity

In the 1980s, as the Seattle DeafBlind community grew, the collapse of the world became a collective problem, rather than an individual problem, and pressure was exerted on local infrastructure to adapt. Claims to public transit, telecommunications, and public education were formulated on behalf of a new political group (i.e. neither "Deaf" nor "Blind" but "DeafBlind"). As part of that process, a set of DeafBlind identities crystalized, which were legible within the larger socio-political system (Chapter 5).

Embracing one of the available DeafBlind identities led to significant improvements in the lives of those I interviewed in 2006, who had moved to Seattle 10–20 years prior. When I asked people if they were ever tempted to go back to their home towns, the answer was, without exception, "No." The most common reason given for this was the availability of services, funded by the state of Washington and supported by a strong, institutionally embedded network of service providers, such as specially trained interpreters, guides, and legal advocates. Going back home would mean relinquishing those services, which would restrict action to such an extent that it would be impossible, as Janet explained, to "have a life":

> Seattle is my home for sure. I'm not leaving. I miss my family in Nebraska, but there are no services there for DeafBlind people, so many of them are isolated, not at all interacting with society. They're very behind there. There is not a lot of education or awareness. DeafBlind people there mostly just stay at home alone, not doing much. I was very lucky to come to Seattle where things are much further along for DeafBlind people.

Janet, like many others, felt fortunate. Being in a place with services meant that action was less restricted, and life was, once again, possible.

The first step toward experiencing those benefits, Janet explained, was getting past a state of "denial" and embracing a DeafBlind identity. When I asked her what might have happened if she had stayed in Nebraska, she said:

> If I had stayed in Nebraska, I would be in denial. I wouldn't have learned Braille, I wouldn't have learned how to use a cane, I would have probably had less and less friends as the years went on […]. It would have been a lot more work on my part to live there, and ultimately, I think I would have been extremely lonely. I'm really happy I moved to Seattle where I could grow, and learn new things. I came to be a confident person here who has accepted my identity, and who has a community, and a life.

In another interview, a Deaf sighted employee of the DeafBlind program at the Lighthouse in the early 1980s also identified "denial" as a root problem, which prevented people from embracing their DeafBlind identity. He explained that as the community began to grow:

> some were very resistant to the idea that they were blind. They were always saying that they were only "a little bit blind," and they insisted that they were Deaf. They wanted to keep communicating the way they did when they were sighted, which was fine, but as soon as they were put in a position to communicate directly with another DeafBlind person, they didn't want anything to do with it. They just really had a lot of resistance to changing the way they communicated.

Denial was framed by both sighted and DeafBlind people as a kind of psychological resistance to reality, which was usually tied to trauma, fear, stigma, or all three. Kathryn, for example, said that DeafBlind people in her Deaf school were picked on and even beaten up, and this caused lasting damage, which made it more difficult for her to embrace a DeafBlind identity:

> When I was a senior at the Deaf school, I was on the volleyball team. I was a star player. I was chosen by the school to join the team. I was very involved, and things were going along OK. Then one game, we were playing against another Deaf school, and it was a really close game. We were neck and neck—they would gain the lead, then we would come back, and toward the end of the game, it was a tie. The ball came over the net, and somehow, my mind couldn't understand what I was seeing and it went right over my head. Their team won. So I was disappointed, but I had to accept that we had lost. Then, once we were off the court, a player from our team came up to me and said she didn't like to lose, and then she beat me up. She did it because I couldn't see the ball, and so I contributed to our team losing. That was a terrible day that I will never forget.

Events like this continued to happen until Kathryn's parents decided she should see an eye doctor. She describes, like many others, the crude way in which she was informed of her impending blindness by the doctor, and the effect it had on her:

> I went in for all day testing. I didn't like it at all. No interpreter was provided. The ADA hadn't been established yet at that time, in 1977. [...] There was no law that said you had to provide an interpreter. So I spent the whole time tapping people on the shoulder and asking them, "What did you say? What did you say?" My parents and the doctors were all standing there discussing the situation. My parents said they would tell me later. I had very limited knowledge about Usher Syndrome. The doctor said, "You. One day you will be blind." I was shocked. I didn't understand why he thought I would become blind when I was older. I thought to myself, "I can't accept blindness." I had already grown up sighted for 19 years, experiencing the world that way. So when I found out I had Ushers, I just couldn't accept it. And the way the doctor told me in no uncertain terms, "You will be blind one day." [...] If only that doctor had described these things to me properly. [...] Before I met with that doctor, I was talkative, social, but after that, I became very reserved.

When Kathryn moved to Seattle, she started to face her fear of tactile communication. Nevertheless, there was an important line that she still would not cross. Although she learned to communicate with people who received ASL signs through touch, or "tactile people," actually becoming a tactile person remained unimaginable:

> I had to accept touch. I had to learn how to interact, and communicate with tactile people, but it was all one-way. They would use tactile reception, but I wouldn't. I hadn't practiced, so I didn't know how. Really that doctor [...] ruined it for me. That experience was so traumatic that even after 33 years, it's still hard to get over it.

Kathryn summed up her fear of going tactile, even after she had moved to Seattle, as a sign of her denial. She found the thought of going blind so terrifying that she never accepted that it was happening. Moving to Seattle was a sort of compromise. The systems that were in place, on the one hand, required her to be "DeafBlind," On the other hand, being DeafBlind within those systems meant compensating for vision, thereby maintaining a fundamentally visual orientation to the world rather than transitioning to a more tactile way of life:

> After I moved here, I wouldn't say I made wonderful progress. You really have to understand yourself. I needed to know who I really was as a DeafBlind person. I had

to accept that. So between then and now, I've been doing better, but there are still some things that I haven't faced. For instance, I should be using a cane all the time, every day, but I don't. When I look outside, and notice that it is a bright day, I think, "I don't need a cane! I'll be fine!" Tactile reception is another example. I don't need tactile reception. I can still see what people are saying when they sign through my tunnel of vision. So that's what I mean by "denial."

Denial was often framed like this—as an unwillingness to accept a self-evident truth. However, as we will learn in the next chapter, overcoming denial and embracing identity may have obscured more than it revealed. Ultimately, this was not how cycles of collapse ended in the Seattle DeafBlind community.

3.2 What Identity Obscures

In the immediate aftermath of collapse (if all goes well), there will be two main choices: Take on a new identity, to which resources are tethered, or cope more directly with your environment, now deformed, disordered, or replaced by something wholly unfamiliar. Select the first choice, and there will be planning and paperwork, followed by silence. Select the second choice, and there will be a junk yard, which may contain (some of) the contents of your former life. Wandering around, hoping to find something (anything!) you can work with, is what it means to start with affordances.

Recall from Chapter 1 that the idea of "affordances" was introduced by the ecological psychologist, James J. Gibson (2015 [1977]: 119–136). According to Gibson, organisms interacting with their environment learn to recognize objects not by discriminating properties such as size, shape, or texture, but by perceiving affordances. A surface can be climbed on insofar as it is "climb-on-able." It can be walked on insofar as it is "walk-on-able." So while the surface of a lake has certain abstract properties like flatness, extension, and non-rigidity, it has very different affordances for a human and a water bug (Gibson 2015 [1977]: 127).

Under routine circumstances, affordances appear to the organism as features of the things themselves, which call forth action in particular ways. As Gibson puts it: "The postbox 'invites' the mailing of a letter, the handle 'wants to be grasped,' and things 'tell us what to do with them'" (Gibson 2015 [1977]: 138). Insofar as the equipment is up and running, you go about your business, barely paying attention to the fact that the environment is throwing out messages, which you can perceive and are equipped to act on. When the world collapses, things go silent—nothing tells you what to do with it. In cases like this, where the organism-environment relation is disrupted, Gibson points out that new sets of affordances, or "niches," can be discovered (121):

> The natural environment offers many ways of life, and different animals have different ways of life. The niche implies a kind of animal, and the animal implies a kind of niche. Note the complementarity of the two. But note also that the environment as a whole with its unlimited possibilities existed prior to animals.

In other words, there is an excess of possibilities in the environment. If one collection of affordances fails the organism, another can be uncovered: "[T]here may be many offerings of the environment that have *not* been taken advantage of, that is, niches not yet occupied" (121).

However, this abundance of possibilities is not readily accessible to individuals, moment to moment, since the interpretation of affordances on any one occasion (particularly for humans) is influenced by how affordances have been interpreted in the past, e.g. in a given social group, locality, or historical period. The fact that affordances are not only perceived but also learned means that there is some circularity and a tendency toward homogenization. The environment is organized by patterns of perception and interaction, and also reinforces and shapes those patterns (Lynch 1960; Bourdieu 1970; Simmel 1971; Panofsky 1973; Hanks 1990; Benjamin 1999; Hull 2012; Keane 2014; Throop 2016). For example, Gibson discusses the meaning of a "seat" (120):

> The human species in some cultures has the habit of sitting as distinguished from kneeling or squatting. If a surface of support [is] knee-high above the ground, it affords sitting on. We call it a *seat*. . . .

A sitting culture values seats—stumps, ledges, benches, and of course chairs. Chairs are manufactured in great number. The mass production of chairs, and their placement all across the landscape, reinforces a culture of sitting (as opposed to kneeling or squatting). Over time, certain seating arrangements become conventional within rooms, certain layouts of rooms within houses become common in certain places and periods of time; There are patterns in terms of how houses within neighborhoods are arranged, and so on. Each of these arrangements is a "collection of affordances." They are part of a niche, which is not discovered anew each time an individual stumbles upon it. People in sitting cultures are socialized from an early age to sit in seats and to do so in particular ways. As processes like this transpire, an abundance of affordances in the environment are narrowed to some limited sub-set.

Within any cultural group, there is also variation. The narrowing and homogenization of human-environment relations therefore affects some more than others, and in different ways. Gibson notes, for example, that "[k]nee high for a child is not the same as knee-high for an adult, so the affordance is relative to the size of the individual" (120). Furthermore, we rarely sit merely to sit. We sit in order to engage in some other activity, such as conversation, playing cards, rest, or reading. Therefore, homogenization will affect groups differently, depending on how those activities are routinely structured across the group. Variation can also be observed in different geographical regions and historical periods. For example, Edward T. Hall argues that those who have been socialized in North America move through, and interact with, the world in ways that hide its tactile affordances. He asks us to "[t]hink for a moment how young children and infants reach, grasp, fondle, and mouth everything, and how many years are required to train children to subordinate the world of touch to the visual world." This process, he argues, is amplified by our interactions with the manufactured environment. Cars, chairs, and other kinesthetically un-engaging vessels populating the North American landscape isolate us from thermal, olfactory, and tactile affordances in our environment.

Given this state of affairs, DeafBlind people in North America have two choices: Stick with the layout as it is or find new ways of interacting with the environment. If you choose to embrace an established, legible identity, the furniture stays where it is. You sit in the furniture like you were taught to, and if that arrangement is not effective for carrying on a conversation, accommodations can be requested on the basis of one's identity. With accommodations, an approximation of the world can be thrown up any time it is needed. This was the approach taken by the Seattle DeafBlind community for the first 30 years of its history. If a DeafBlind member of the community couldn't see what other people were saying, someone would tell them what was said. If they weren't sure what kind of room they were in, someone would describe it.

Identities are locked into a lot of structure. Choosing to start with affordances instead means letting structure fall away, and with it many things that have felt like, or promise to be, lifelines—all of the accommodations, services, and supports. Starting with affordances is a difficult move not only because it usually involves a significant departure from norms and standards, but also because hidden affordances are, by definition, unknown and difficult to imagine. Understandably, then, the Seattle DeafBlind community went further and further down the well-trodden path of identity, and as they did, the weight of *existential strain* was increasingly felt.

3.3 Existential Strain

Strain involves actions that may be effective, but not appropriate, appropriate but not effective, or neither appropriate nor effective (Kockelman 2006a: 39). Strain can occur when an instrument is not designed well (2006a: 44); when a group of people rejects standards of appropriateness and prioritizes efficacy, as when skateboarders redefine the functions of public architecture: "sidewalks, walls, ramps, curbs," and so on (Kockelman 2006a: 41); and when a group of people adheres to the normative use of an instrument, despite the fact that it is not effective for them when used that way (Kockelman 2006a: 41). Strain is part of life, but if there is a general trend, where the human-environment relation is disrupted and norms and standards maintain their hold to the exclusion of efficacy, strain will likely turn to collapse. The boundary between strain and collapse is breached when action becomes so restricted by norms and standards, that it is no longer possible to be who you are. This is precisely what happened for members of the Seattle DeafBlind community when sighted standards of conduct were maintained to such an extent that for thirty years, a visual language was the primary mode of communication for a group of people who can't see.

But why would anyone submit themselves to norms and standards that make communication, navigation, and ultimately existence itself impossible? Kathryn's story suggests that one motivating factor is the powerful stigma that accrues to "blindness," not as a positive identity, but as a condition that thwarts appropriate, Deaf conduct. Evading stigma involves either: (1) demonstrating that one can behave "appropriately," *despite* blindness; or (2) stretching the boundaries around sighted notions of appropriateness to make slightly strange behavior more acceptable. The first option depends on sight to some degree. People who are fully blind can no longer act as if they are sighted, while people who are partially sighted might be able to. Asking sighted people to accommodate on a case-by-case basis, leads to idiosyncratic attempts to modify social norms according to individual "needs." Lee, one of the leaders of the protactile movement, reflected on such attempts.

> A month ago, I was with [Janet], and I ended up interpreting what people were saying because I wasn't lost, but she was totally lost and frustrated, and [she was] complaining that people weren't following all of the many ridiculous rules that you

have to follow to make visual communication with her possible. She put it in terms of "respect." She said people weren't respecting her. They shouldn't walk quickly by—it's confusing. They should stand at the right distance. They should sign slowly [...]. It is not reasonable to expect people to do that, and they don't. So the result is that she's left out, and is getting more and more frustrated as time goes by [...].

Lee and her collaborators argued that these kinds of interventions cannot happen on an individual level. With the inception of the protactile movement, a third option was revealed: Give up on sighted notions of appropriateness altogether and find an effective way of being in the world that does not involve vision at all. Prior to the protactile movement, that option may have led somewhere wonderful, but once you got there, you would be alone. The limited options DeafBlind people had all involved embracing a DeafBlind identity, and yet embracing a DeafBlind identity turned out to be a temporary fix. Denial followed people to Seattle and caused problems long after their DeafBlind identities were established.

For example, Felicia had already been through an ordeal in Oregon before relocating to Seattle. When she arrived, she found that there were two main options for how she could be DeafBlind. She could be a "tactile person," which at the time meant placing her hands on the hands of the signer as they produced signs in ASL (a visual language). The other viable option was being a "tunnel-vision person," which involved asking others to sign in a smaller space, moving back to see more of what people were saying, working with interpreters to manage group communication settings, and so on. She realized right away that being a tunnel-vision person was preferable. They were the ones with more active social lives, better jobs, and overall, a higher quality of life. She therefore moved quickly to embrace her identity as a "tunnel-vision" person.

Some years later, though, people started telling Felicia she should "switch to tactile." Her inability to do this, they said, was affecting her relationships, her effectiveness at work, her ability to be a mother, and nearly every other aspect of her life. It was then, she told me, that the life she had assembled upon her arrival in Seattle started falling apart all over again:

My ex-husband told me that I was missing what he was saying. He would get angry and frustrated, saying that I didn't understand what he was saying and he blamed it on me not being able to read his face. At work people started telling me that I was misunderstanding. People were very blunt with me. My boss at work started asking me all the time if I understood what she was saying. I had to take all of that in for a while, and then finally someone sat me down and said, "Your eyes are getting worse. You have to do something." And I didn't want to believe it. I told them it wasn't true. I mean, I could see, but I missed so much. My vision couldn't pick up facial expression, which was a major problem. For example, when I looked at my own baby, I thought she was laughing but really she was crying. My ex-husband would yell at me and say, "You thought the baby was laughing?? No! She was crying!" But I didn't see the tears. I was really beside myself, but I held it all in. My marriage was a complete disaster. Communication was only one of the reasons. So communication started failing all the time, and I was in denial, which was a terrible combination. […] I have to admit, for a long time I pretended to understand what people were saying to me. It's terrible, but I did. I'm not proud of that at all.

Felicia maintained her tunnel-vision DeafBlind identity as long as she could. Sighted norms and standards maintained their hold and eventually action became so restricted that it was no longer possible for her to be who she was. Being a DeafBlind person in a visual world depends on being able to take on roles in ways that are legible to sighted people. Felicia was, among other things, a professional at work and a wife and mother at home. As she slowly lost her sight, she must have adjusted along the way, but then all at once she found herself locked out of those roles. She told me, "My husband was very controlling. He thought I couldn't be a mother." Her boss was asking if she had understood after every exchange, which suggested to Felicia that she was no longer trusted to do her job. Her life was falling apart. You can blame Felicia for not switching to tactile sooner, but people who did fared no better.

For example, Adrijana started perceiving ASL through touch early, before she "needed" to. But when she moved to Seattle in 1997, she was struck by how dependent everyone was on interpreters. She thought that being a tactile person meant that she would experience the kind of immediacy she had enjoyed as a Deaf sighted person. But in Seattle, she said:

There was no one to talk to! Everyone was busy chatting with their [interpreters]. I started to feel like, "Who am I? Why did I even move here to Seattle? I'm from a Deaf world where communication is direct and unmediated. Now everything seems wrong. Like I took a step backwards into a hearing environment."

Lee, who had moved to Seattle in 2001, shared Adrijana's sense of disappointment. She noted that going tactile was very clearly:

something negative that people gave into; something that would draw sympathy and looks of consoling understanding. It was not something people went into with positive aspirations or enthusiasm.

In many of the interviews I conducted, becoming a tactile person—an inevitability for everyone—was as Lee describes. For example, Susan said that one day she was at a staff meeting at the Lighthouse and she was watching an interpreter visually, just like she always did. At some point, someone said, "Susan? Are you going to answer?" And she realized that she had been missing what the person was saying. Before that, she thought she had been catching everything. To clarify, someone tried to communicate with her through touch and she pulled away, asking what the person was doing. By this time, she was certain everyone was watching and she was embarrassed. Tactile communication wasn't helpful for her because she hadn't developed the skill. She didn't want to put her lack of skill on display and at the same time, she didn't want to take that step toward becoming a tactile person. She was trapped between two DeafBlind identities, neither of which seemed to offer a feasible way forward.

Eventually, Susan learned how to receive ASL signs through touch, but this only led to new problems. She explained that often, DeafBlind people would say, "Susan? Is that you communicating through touch with me? Your eyes have gotten worse!" That kind of response was hard for her. Susan said that switching to tactile was a necessary change, but overall it was depressing. Right away she realized that she couldn't participate in groups the same way. For example, at the Lighthouse for the Blind where she worked, there were two separate lunch groups. If you were still a tunnel-vision person, you could eat with the other tunnel-vision people. Once you went tactile, though, you had to either switch to the tactile group, or be left out of conversations. Susan's friends were all still in the tunnel-vision group, but that was no longer a feasible communication situation for her so she saw less and less of them. She also described a process of increasing dependence on interpreters, where the quality of her day, or a meeting she attended, or her level of interest in a person she was communicating with depended on whether her interpreter was tired, whether they knew her preferences or not, and so on. She said, all in all, going from "tunnel vision" to "tactile" had been a negative experience for her.

The idea of "denial" suggests that people like Susan are resistant to reality, but her story and many others like it suggest that putting off the transition from *tunnel-vision* to *tactile* reflected a perfectly solid grasp of reality in Seattle at that time. Tunnel-vision people had more access to resources, they were the first to learn of any new information circulating, they had better jobs, were invited to better parties. In general, they had better lives. People avoided tactility because it opened onto a path of social demotion, isolation, and increased dependence on sighted people.

Reflecting on this problem later, two key leaders of the protactile movement, Adrijana and Lee, argued that the problem was not tactility itself, but the fact that the community's standards of conduct were *sighted* standards. Underneath "DeafBlind" identities like "tactile" and "tunnel vision," were *sighted* roles, and the actions deemed appropriate and effective for taking on those roles. For example, as part of my fieldwork in 2010, I attended bi-weekly classes where groups of DeafBlind people gathered to exchange information and socialize and there were often presentations. In venues like these, DeafBlind people rarely communicated directly with one another. Instead, sighted ways of organizing communication were maintained and accommodations were provided.

For sighted people, a "presenter" is a person who stands on a stage and addresses many audience members at once. When this is the base assumption, the number and positioning of sighted relays becomes complicated very quickly. For example, on one occasion, a DeafBlind man was standing on a stage preparing to give a presentation. Each DeafBlind audience member listened to the presentation through an interpreter. A sighted person stood behind the DeafBlind presenter. Any time the presenter rotated his body so he wasn't facing the audience, his orientation was adjusted by the sighted person, manually. If a person in the audience asked a question, the presenter used his small tunnel of vision to receive the question. However, he wouldn't look at the person asking the question directly because he couldn't find them efficiently. With a small tunnel of vision, searching for the signer takes time. Instead, the person asking the question would stand up so all of the interpreters in the room could see them. From there, an interpreter on stage would copy the question. Next, an interpreter seated at the base of the stage facing the presenter would copy the copy of the question, at which point, the presenter would have access to the audience-member's question. All questions and comments from the audience were funneled through just that one person, which reduced the amount of time spent searching since the presenter would always know where to look.

Complex networks of mediation like this were established—not as a means of becoming tactile, but as a means of stretching the visual world as far as it could possibly go. The enemy was blindness, not the primacy of visuality or the "distantism" it engenders (Clark 2017). As more and more members of the community became blind, problems with this approach became apparent. Prior to the protactile movement, the response to vision loss was always an increase in mediation strategies aimed at maintaining as much access as possible to the visual world. However, performing an action in a way that is appropriate for taking up a sighted role, without being able to see how others perform those actions, makes it increasingly difficult to know an action will be interpreted as intended. The feedback loop is broken, and this leads to "commitment issues," another sign that whatever order there is in the world might be resting on unstable ground.

3.4 Commitment Issues

To commit is to internalize, and therefore be able to anticipate, the meaning or effect of your actions (Kockelman 2006a: 61). This applies, for example, to the way an utterance represents some type of action (e.g. "Hi!" represents a "greeting"), and also the way an utterance causes some sort of affective response, or "interpretant," such as an increase in metabolism, a blush, a feeling of pain, or a feeling of being off balance (Kockelman 2005: 274). Adjusting, clarifying, or repairing misconstruals of communicative intent is part of life. However, collapse may be on the horizon if, as a rule, the effects of your actions are misconstrued.

When the world is up and running, actions are controlled and purposeful behaviors that result in the realization of an instrument, another action, incorporation by a role or identity, or an utterance that represents it (Kockelman 2006a: 44). For example, carpentry (action), could realize a table (instrument). Throwing a ball to another person (action) might lead that person to throw the ball back to you (another action), in which case, this second action contextualizes and incorporates the first action. Now you're playing a "game of catch." In the context of a game, this kind of action might be incorporated into a role, such as "catcher," and if you take on such roles habitually, they might be incorporated into an identity, such as "athlete." You can't have a role if you never do anything, and you can't have an identity if you never do anything habitually in ways that align with normative frames for interpreting whatever it is that you are doing.

Accounting more specifically for language-use, to "commit" is to internalize, and therefore be able to anticipate, the meaning or effect of your utterances from the perspective of the person to whom they are addressed, including not only representational effects (e.g. an utterance produced in response to your utterance), but also affective effects (e.g. a person registers your utterance through an increase in body temperature, visible as blood flow in the face). Calibrating one's utterances to achieve purposeful effects requires that over many instances of communicating, these sorts of effects are perceptible to the speaker. The effects themselves, however, are not purposeful or controlled. They are not things we do, but things that happen to us. At most, we experience affective responses like these as something we must resist, or manage (Kockelman 2005: 274–275). In addition to representational and affective responses, there are "energetic" responses. These involve physical reactions like "flinching at the sound of a gun" or "tiptoeing on a creaky floor" (Kockelman 2005: 275). In contrast to affective responses, these are things we do (they don't just happen to us), but unlike representational effects, we do not cause them in an entirely controlled or purposeful manner. It is crucial to note that the same kind of dependencies and inclusions obtain here: Representational effects depend on and include affective and energetic effects. You can't guarantee that your utterance will be interpreted in the way you hoped it would, unless you have a sense of how all three effects interact across contexts. Over time, one develops a feeling for relations across domains, which gives rise to dispositions in how we speak, or act, more generally. In other words, dispositions to act in particular ways are guided and constrained by our internalized sense of how people will respond along representational, affective, and energetic lines (Kockelman 2005: 277–278).

We exert control, for example, when walking across a creaky floor at night, because we have internalized the "energetic" effect of that action on someone else: One wakes up, startled by the sound. We don't think about it explicitly, and yet, in order to internalize those responses, they must be routinely available in the environment. DeafBlind people who have been spared the experience of living with hearing people slam doors and cupboards, walk confidently across a creaky floor at night, and let the tea kettle whistle for as long as they like. In contrast, DeafBlind people living with hearing people are put in a strange position: they can be expected to internalize energetic effects of their actions, which they, themselves, do not experience.

For example, Julie explained that before she came to Seattle and was still living in Utah she often had to internalize effects that she did not experience. The only language available to her was ASL. "Tactile sign language," as she describes it below, meant tactile reception of ASL. "Beauty" referred to how someone looked not how they felt, and what counted as appropriate behavior presupposed sighted norms as well. When Julie started to lose her vision, she applied her intellect to the problem. She liked the unknown more than most and she figured there must be a way forward. So she started trying things—*tactile things*—with everyone she met. What she encountered was a highly restricted range of intelligibility for anything involving touch. Within those constraints, she explained, there were only a couple of possibilities:

> In Utah, I used tactile sign language, but only with men. Rarely were women comfortable with it. Most of them were concerned about being misconstrued as a

lesbian, and so avoided touching other women in public. The husbands were more than happy to talk, but when it came time for the wives to join the conversation, they always seemed nervous and they always refused. So I generally ended up conversing with husbands and ignoring wives. It's not that women and men saw the situation differently, but the men looked at it as something they could take advantage of and the women didn't. In order for me to avoid social isolation, I had to be pretty all the time. That was how I could relate with men because wanting to touch someone, for them, had to do with how pretty that person was. For me it was a matter of basic communication. So my access to communication was based on a fundamental misunderstanding about touch. DeafBlind people in Utah who were not attractive stayed home. They were socially isolated. Focusing on my looks was something I regarded as pure survival. And it wasn't just my appearance. I also wanted to make good money because I knew that being more materialistic, having nice things, would also attract people. And I was lucky that I had a brain. I took advantage of the fact that people were attracted to my mind.

This was not a way of being, exactly, but it wasn't social isolation, either. Julie resigned herself to this limited way of interacting with others for the sake of survival. This time in her life, she told me, was frustrating. Any attempt at forward motion brought her back to where she had started. She knew what she had to do. She had to extend tactility into domains of life not normally associated with touch, such as routine communication. But communicating effectively required that she communicate "inappropriately," and this made it impossible for her to commit (Kockelman 2006a: 61). The things she needed to do just to interact with others were interpreted in ways that she not only didn't intend but that she actively resisted. Every time she tried to touch someone for purposes of routine communication, the interaction quickly narrowed to one of two predictable frames: Either the unintended appearance of "homosexual" flirtation or the unintended appearance of "heterosexual" flirtation (the former less appropriate to the people around her than the latter). Many DeafBlind people who moved to Seattle from elsewhere had parallel experiences. They describe the places they came from as lacking basic necessities; they couldn't live there. Being unable to commit in basic communicative acts was a significant part of the problem.

Upon relocating to Seattle, it was possible to be intelligible as a DeafBlind person and, even, as a specific kind of DeafBlind person. However, working with interpreters involved complex participant frames, even in relatively simple circumstances. When an entire room is filled with DeafBlind people, each of whom has been assigned an interpreter, participant frames grow excessively complex and commitment issues are encountered once again. An interpreter who had been involved in the community since the 1980s when group communication was new associated this with what she called a "turn-taking" problem. She explained in an interview that back then:

> [o]ne of the most memorable problems was turn-taking. DeafBlind people didn't understand how to do it, and interpreters too. Interpreters were there for short periods of time [as students], then they moved away, or whatever, so people would learn, but then there were new people who didn't know yet, and there were so many confusions. Someone would say something, and the person would be confused about why THAT person (the interpreter) would be saying that thing. And the interpreter would try to explain, "It's not ME. It's [Randy] saying that. I'm just interpreting what he's saying," and it was really a challenge.

Early on in Seattle's history, this was a common problem. People would mistake the interpreter (animator) for the signer (author) of the utterance, and communication would go circular. In one situation:

> Ronald stood up in front of everyone, and signed "READY?" to his interpreter, Rose, and [Rose] said "READY?" in English. Then his interpreter signed what Rose said back to Ronald instead of saying "YES," and it just went on like that in a potentially endless loop. Until finally Rose said, "DO NOT SIGN READY! SIGN YES!" [Laughs.] We could still be there if Rose hadn't said something.

In order for DeafBlind people to communicate with one another at that point in the community's history, and especially in groups, sighted interpreters were necessary (Chapter 5). However, the presence of interpreters introduced an additional layer of commitment issues. In this particular case, the pronominal systems of English and ASL were set to retrieve values from participant frameworks that only some participants had unrestricted access to. For DeafBlind people who were not relying on vision, the "person currently speaking," for example, was their interpreter by default. In order to generate alternate retrievable values, proper names had to be rigidly associated with the speaker of every utterance—a habit that each new interpreter and DeafBlind member of the community had to learn and habituate to.

By the mid-1990s, when I entered the community as an undergraduate student studying interpreting, these issues had been worked out. Conventions were in place for smooth turn-taking, people understood how many different participant frameworks worked via interpreters, there were options for how DeafBlind people could participate, and they started to take intelligibility for granted. Only when people traveled outside of Seattle after living there for some time, did interpretations of actions once again become precarious, reminding them what they now had.

Helen, for example, had been in Seattle for years when she and I traveled to Arizona for a short weekend trip. On our first day there, we went out. It was a sunny summer day. She wanted a milkshake and I wanted coffee. Helen is older than I am and uses a cane. When we walk together, we touch each other to coordinate our movements and to converse. I wondered how people in Arizona might make sense of us. Would they recognize the cane and assume that a blind person was involved? When they noticed the "hand holding" would they consider the possibility that tactile communication was taking place? I was curious about the differences but Helen was anxious. Any time intelligibility was destabilized, a previous life was conjured in which the only roles available to her were based on a fundamental misunderstanding of her actions.

As we set out on our excursion in Arizona, things immediately went the wrong way. Helen and I had routine ways of interacting, which were effective and appropriate in Seattle. This was the case not only in DeafBlind community spaces but also in particular neighborhoods in Seattle, where people were used to seeing DeafBlind people. We wanted to maintain that sense of intelligibility and go about our business, committed to what we were doing. Maybe, if we projected confidence, people would see that we had a way to be, even if they weren't sure what it was. But then at the ice cream place they made too much, so they gave Helen an extra cup. Now she had one hand for the cane, one for the milkshake, and no hands for the second cup, for communication, or for maintaining contact with me while walking. I tried to help. I carried the cane under one arm, and held the extra cup in my hand. Helen used one hand for keeping track of me and one hand for her milkshake. All of the possible cues were being obscured and tension was building.

Our plan was still in motion. We were on our way across the street to the coffee place, where we would soon be able to sit down, talk, and enjoy our beverages. While we were waiting at the crosswalk, I told Helen that I still wanted to go to the cafe across the street, but I wanted beer instead of coffee. She responded negatively to this idea, yelling, "Great! Now I'll be your child!" In fact, it is not uncommon for DeafBlind people who are older than the sighted person they are with to be mistaken for the sighted person's child, and the beverages one chooses can take on a decisive role in such readings. The stakes were too high. Any action might set off some unwieldy chain of interpretations, which had the potential to reduce existence, once again, to mere survival.

Standing on the corner, we reflected on the absurdity of the image we were inhabiting together, evacuated of any relevant roles or identities. We burst into laughter, the cane still wrenched up under my arm, sticking out almost into traffic. What could we possibly *be* in public? Maybe Helen was right. The closest possibility was an adult with the mental capacity of a child (which would be a reasonable explanation for the milk shake, the beer, and the "hand holding" while crossing the street). Over the course of our visit, we returned to that joke. It was a serious joke about the hazards of being hard to see. Those hazards, which multiply the further one gets from Seattle, lead to anxieties about doing what one must to exist.

Commitment is always problematic, hence the ubiquity of adjustment, clarification, re-framing, and repair in everyday interactions (e.g. Sidnell 2015: 180). However, when unintelligibility is the most or *only* predictable outcome, meaningful action will be reliably thwarted, roles will be out of reach, and existence will be undermined or terminally restricted.

3.5 Keeping Things Life-Like

In Seattle, people didn't mistake your interpreter for your mother, nor did they mistake basic communicative touch for sexual interest. However, once people settled into their new DeafBlind identities, whether they were "tunnel-vision" or "tactile" people, the signs of collapse would eventually resurface and existence would, once again, feel fragile. During six months of fieldwork conducted in 2006 and 2008, I became keenly aware of the mounting pressure exerted on language. Descriptions of the world were expected to stand in for the world, but could not effectively do so. As a result, life was strained and it was hard to commit. Things were on the brink of collapse (again) and as people crept closer and closer to the unknown, it seemed that it would be up to language to keep things looking life-like.

In the spring of 2008, I spent a lot of time with Helen. One of the activities Helen and I enjoyed together was "people watching." We would walk around in the city together, pausing for "snapshots" of what I saw. If I described something Helen was interested in, she would ask questions, and in the back and forth an image of the environment would form. I ended up doing things like tracing a stream of sunlight into the squinting eyes of a driver as his car moved slowly by or describing a pale-skinned woman draped in a thin, black dress, sulking on the giant billboard above. One time, Helen and I were sitting against the back wall at a public event. I found two people whom I could eavesdrop on and I started relaying their conversation to Helen. She stopped me and said she wasn't interested in people's conversations: she wanted to know how they were holding their heads, what they were doing with their feet and their eyes, if there were flashes of discomfort or amusement. She would say things like: "Describe all of the eyebrows you see." Or: "Are the hands in this room pocketed?" Though her focus of attention was always shifting, one thing was consistent. She was not interested in my take on things. She wanted me to provide her with an excess of descriptive detail, which she could interpret and evaluate according to her own criteria. And she wasn't interested in people per se. She was reading the ambient environment off of their responses to it, and to do that effectively what she needed from me were details—as specific and as numerous as possible.

Helen wasn't the only one. At that point in the history of the community, sighted people were being treated as a portal to the present. That posed a challenge for interpreters, who were being asked to generate descriptions that were as concrete and indeterminate as reality. The technique for achieving that was similar to what Roland Barthes calls the "reality effect," (1984: 141–154) which in literature involves writing in superfluous detail, drawing attention to things that are, as he says, "neither incongruous nor significant" (ibid.: 142). Barthes argues that such details, only when provided in great excess, can end up conveying something of the character or atmosphere of a place. Each thing is insignificant, but the cumulative effect of all of that insignificance is a sense that you are there. So in lieu of reality interpreters were being trained to generate a *reality effect*. This pushed language to some kind of limit. Interpreters were scrambling to generate realist portraits of reality in real time. In the end, though, the world was always going flat, despite every attempt to keep it looking life-like.

Recall that our dispositions to act are guided and constrained by our internalized sense of how people will respond—not only representational responses, such as an utterance, but also affective and energetic responses, such as blushing or walking with more controlled movements (Kockelman 2005: 277–278 and see Chapter 1). While sighted interpreters tended to focus on what people were saying to one another, Helen was more interested in affective and energetic effects, perhaps because in order to commit, she needed to know what responses were likely and possible. Since she couldn't perceive responses of any kind directly, she asked me to describe them, but describing affective and energetic effects turns them into representations. Representational effects include and depends on affective and energetic effects. When language was divorced from its effects for extended periods of time, things fell apart.

The foundation fell out from under representation, just like it fell out from under everything else because norms for DeafBlind interaction and communication were established by sighted people who perceived affordances in the environment in visual ways, including the affordances of language. The disposition to adhere to normative standards of appropriate conduct kept DeafBlind people from findings effective ways to interact with their environment. Therefore, even though vision was the one thing that was *not* shared across the group, a visual language—ASL—became the main instrument through which, the environment was perceived.

In 2006, I attended a workshop for sighted interpreters on "visual analysis," which was a collection of methods meant to push language into the realm of visual perception, ultimately substituting for it. One such method, which was similar to the technique I had learned from Helen, was called "passive seeing." Lee, the DeafBlind instructor, talked about this as a mode of attention, saying:

> The goal is more to evoke an image that the DeafBlind person can then interpret. Tap into the mood of the place, the passive aspects. Fill in the background, the texture of the scene, so the DeafBlind person can be free to make their own decisions about how to interact with their world. You can't substitute your opinion for visual analysis and expect that to be informative.

Lee and the other DeafBlind instructor went on to perform a role-playing exercise that illustrated the difference between conveying an "opinion" such as, "That man over there is friendly," and conducting "visual analysis," where details of the scene are conveyed in such a way that more than just "looking-at" would become possible. The role-play in the workshop was set in a restaurant and the instructors were playing the role of patrons. They were interacting, but saying very little to one another. The students were instructed to ignore the dialog and attend to the "feeling" of the interaction, which they would be asked to report on later. There were also several DeafBlind people participating in the workshop who were watching the role-play via sighted interpreters. A few moments into the exercise, one of those interpreters interrupted the role-play to explain that without dialog or any notable events there was nothing to interpret. The instructors explained that the point of the workshop was to see that when nothing is being said, the real work begins. Some examples they gave were the direction and consistency of eye-gaze; details about clothing, shoes, and jewelry, including the way they move and are adjusted, and the rhythmic tapping of a foot. These are particularities of setting that rarely make their way into interpreters' descriptions.

Adrijana and Lee were trying to recover these details via a special kind of evocative description. However, evocation presupposes a world and memories of it. DeafBlind people who acquire ASL as sighted or partially sighted children, make connections on a daily basis between the linguistic system and the visual world where it is used. However, if their vision deteriorates and their "tactile scope" (Clark 2015) does not grow, experiences in the world become more restricted over time, memories begin to fade, and language no longer calls anything to mind. In 2006, for example, I videorecorded dyads composed of one DeafBlind person and one sighted interpreter while they walked around downtown Seattle, exploring the city. I walked in front of them with a harness attached to my torso and a pole attached to the harness, which extended up and out. A camera was mounted at the top of the pole and rotated backward, facing the dyad behind me. As I mentioned in Chapter 1, one of those recorded interactions involved a sighted interpreter describing a sculpture in downtown Seattle to a DeafBlind man whom I call Roman. The sculpture is a man, about two stories high, whose arm and fist move up and down, hammering in slow-motion. The interpreter starts with a closed fist, which is a conventional handshape in ASL. The fist represents the head of the hammer. Roman places one hand on top of the interpreter's fist as he moves it slowly toward his own palm, which Roman is also touching. The interpreter's fist comes in contact with his own palm (like a hammer hitting a surface), and then moves slowly back up again. He repeats that motion several times. The interpreter then points to where the sculpture is to link the description of the referent to the referent.

This is a perfectly conventional way of describing a swinging hammer in ASL, and yet Roman seems confused by it. After a few seconds of searching for the referent and apparently failing to locate it, he says, "I remember I saw that sculpture about ten years ago." Modes of access that allow the interpreter to link the description to the referent are tenuous for Roman. He is relying on faded, flat memories and cannot conjure the sculpture's towering size, its immutable presence—black against a sharp, gray sky—or the striking temporal juxtaposition of the arm, slowly sliding back and forth, and the fast-paced activity in the city around it. The interpreter's description can only be received by Roman as uprooted and abstract. He understands the "meaning" of the interpreter's words, but he is alienated from the world to which the description articulates.

Adrijana and Lee were trying to prevent problems like this by teaching interpreters to capture particularities. At some point, though, the interpreter's task became ludicrous. Filling in a missing word here or there became replication of entire utterances, which became copies of utterances and non-linguistic communicative cues, which became detailed descriptions of the crowd, the way light interacts with surfaces, the way styles among the youth keep changing. Interpreters were doing cross-sections of rooms, describing whatever they saw lying around: a bunched up purse on the floor, a shiny metal case of lipstick abandoned on the conference table, a fingerprinted leather wallet, a home-made hat. Needless to say, this ambitious program could not be maintained, and even if it could every DeafBlind person I have known eventually loses interest as their concerns and curiosities turn tactile. Representations of the world cannot substitute for the world. We do not infer the world, we exist in our relation to it. Last ditch attempts to prevent the collapse of the world by substituting propositional semiosis for non-propositional semiosis failed, and along the way, there were many signs that it would.

3.6 Signs of Collapse

Collapse is difficult to grasp in part because we do not perceive collapse itself: we perceive *signs* of collapse. In this chapter, I have asked how DeafBlind people in Seattle read the signs prior to the protactile movement. In analyzing this process, I have also extracted some steps, which might help us understand how worlds collapse more generally. First, the equipment breaks down in ways that make it impossible to go on being who you are. To cope with the situation, you take on a new identity, which unlocks some emergency resources. As you apply those resources, though, you find yourself continuing to do what is appropriate for them, not what is effective for you. The situation drags on, and soon things become strained. Strain is a part of life, but at some point you realize that continuing to adhere to these norms and standards will foreclose any possibility of effective action. At this point, the weight of existential strain is felt and commitment issues arise. Commitment is problematic under normal circumstances, but when misconstrual of your actions is all there is, you know that collapse is on the horizon. As a last-ditch effort you might give up on life and settle for just keeping things life-like, and when that fails you return to your memories, until, eventually, those fade too.

In this chapter, I have shown that for many DeafBlind people in Seattle, responding to collapse involved gaining access, via sighted interpreters, to a receding visual world. The first step in that direction was identity. You identify in a certain way and you get resources on that basis. The protactile critique of that has to do with the importance of "direct access" to the world. However, looking closely at the structure of the world as it came apart, we see that the directness or immediacy involved is not, in a strict sense, immediate. It is actually a special kind of non-propositional mediation. In the next chapter, I focus on how, as part of the protactile movement, DeafBlind people began to reverse this process.

4
The Protactile Movement

This chapter is about the early history of the protactile movement in the 2010s in Seattle, Washington. Although there are broader historical frames that must be taken into account (Chapter 2), the inception of the movement can be located between 2006 and 2008 among the staff of the DeafBlind Service Center (DBSC), and in particular among three DeafBlind staff members, whom I call Adrijana, Lee, and Jodi. Recall that in the decades leading up to this moment, two primary ways of being DeafBlind had crystalized. There were "tactile" people who perceived ASL through touch, and there were "tunnel-vision" people, who perceived ASL through a receding tunnel of vision. Adrijana was the first DeafBlind director of DBSC, but beyond this she was a tactile person. Until this moment, those in leadership positions were either sighted or were able to effectively approximate sighted behaviors. It was rare for a tactile person to be in a position of authority.

When Adrijana became the director of DBSC, she explicitly sought to upend this authority structure. She began by uniting tactile and tunnel-vision people to form one coherent community, and turning DeafBlind people into the experts on their own ways of life and forms of communication. Externally, this involved negotiating "duplicate services" with neighboring organizations. If sighted people were teaching a skill such as "tactile communication" at another organization, Adrijana would encourage people to come to DBSC instead and learn those same skills from a DeafBlind teacher. Internally, this involved building capacity among the DBSC staff to create tactile environments and participate in them consistently. While Adirjana tried many strategies—offering incentives, issuing directives, and simply explaining her goal and asking her staff to opt in, she ultimately found that replacing nearly all of DBSC's staff members was the only way forward. She recalled:

> For about two years, there was a lot of instability in the organization. I really wanted to have the right people in there doing a good job because DBSC is an organization that is there for DeafBlind people, and they had to feel comfortable coming in and getting what they needed.

However, it was not at all self-evident how to make DBSC a comfortable and appealing place for DeafBlind people. Experimentation would be required. Adrijana knew that breaking with previously established norms and experimenting with new ways of interacting and communicating would require at least one collaborator with some specific characteristics. They had to be a rule-breaker more than a rule-follower. They had to be critical, but also creative. They had to be persuasive and, crucially, they had to be *tactile*. Lee, who had just moved to Seattle a few years after Adrijana, fit these criteria to a tee, and once she was hired onto DBSC's staff, she became the key collaborator Adrijana needed.

Adrijana and Lee knew that they wanted to change DBSC in some fundamental ways. Though there were many problem areas, they started with DBSC's public image, as compared with other agencies and organizations in Seattle. In particular, they focused on a local non-profit that served Deaf victims of domestic violence and sexual assault called the Abused Deaf Women's Advocacy Service, or "ADWAS." Adrijana explained:

> [ADWAS] is such a popular organization because they're attractive to people. [...] They're an organization of Deaf women, and it is truly a Deaf environment. They don't have phones, they have TTYs (or they did when they started up). Their board is required to know ASL. The Lighthouse was attractive to people because of [their social and community programs]. But where did DBSC fit in? What was so great about DBSC? That was when the notion of "protactile" came up. It started out really vague and narrow. It didn't mean "touch." It meant, more narrowly, communicating through touch. The point was just to change people's attitudes about tactile communication, as a modality, to say there's nothing wrong with it.

Hearing people were actively encouraged to contribute to ADWAS as volunteers, board members, fundraisers, and so on, as long as they adapted to Deaf norms and did not expect Deaf people to adapt to their norms, and this commitment was built into the structure of the organization, concretely speaking. There were no voice telephones in use, no sound-based door bells, and no furniture that blocked visual communication.

Upon entering, one would encounter conversations unfolding in ASL, not a hearing receptionist talking on the phone. The feeling was, as Adrijana noted, this is a place where Deaf people can come in, feel comfortable, and get what they need. A small change, such as an English-speaking receptionist at the front desk, would have undermined efforts to make the organization welcoming and instead might have turned it into a place where Deaf people were merely accommodated. ADWAS had been successful because of the fact that they were a Deaf organization that served Deaf people according to Deaf norms. This extended beyond direct services. For example, their fundraising events took on a life of their own as vibrant sites of Deaf sociality in Seattle. Talk of a more inviting environment for DeafBlind people came about with a model like this in mind, but what would the DeafBlind version be, and what obstacles would need to be overcome to make it a reality?

4.1 "Everything We Touched Froze"

A meeting of staff, board members, and some community members was called early on in Adrijana's tenure to talk about priorities for DBSC's future. In this meeting, "protactile" started out as a slogan that was used to sell DBSC, but at the same time the more substantive idea of a "DeafBlind Friendly Zone" was raised. Adrijana explains:

> We started using the words, but we didn't really know what they meant. What does it mean to have a DeafBlind friendly zone? Well, tactile signing was important, and we just started thinking about things like that, which led to more and more discussion, and over time it kept changing. For example, we started talking about why it was that if two people were talking to each other, and you walked up and put your hands on one of their hands, they would stop talking. Why not continue, so we can listen for a while? We wanted people to get rid of those habits that made it hard for DeafBlind people to move around a room, observing what was going on tactually.

Although it wasn't clear yet what practices might be considered DeafBlind friendly, there were some things that clearly weren't, such as this habit people had of pausing or "freezing" when a DeafBlind person touched them. DBSC's conference rooms, hallways, and offices were populated by people who were frozen, suspended in mid-air. Adrijana said it had an eerie effect. Sometimes, at lunch, for example, she would take a bite and then reach out to feel the other person's hand or arms to see if they were still eating or not. If they weren't eating, she might say something to them. If they were, she might want to feel their hands take the food to their mouths, or maybe their jaw chewing, but every time she put her hands on someone, they would pause, awkwardly, until she removed her hand. If people were standing around talking in the conference room before a meeting, she would approach them, put her hands on one of them, and hope that they would continue signing, so she could tell what they were talking about. Invariably, though, the conversation would stop. Either they would stop moving, as if they didn't know what to do, or they would ask her what she wanted. How was she to know what she wanted if she didn't know what possibilities for wanting there were? How was she supposed to know what possibilities there were, if she couldn't observe activity in her environment?

In the past, this kind of observation was always accomplished with a sighted interpreter, but interpreters were in short supply, and Adrijana often went without one. Furthermore, she didn't think tactile observation was implausible in such situations, but in the larger community frames for interpreting action like this were missing, so when it was done it was confusing, irritating, or on occasion even interpreted as inappropriately sexual. For Adrijana and several of her friends and colleagues, there was a disconnect. In 2006, I conducted two months of fieldwork, and during that time, I lived with Adrijana and her Deaf, sighted husband. They and several of their friends (both sighted and DeafBlind) had intuitively started "observing" the activity around them through touch.

In 2008, I also lived with Adrijana and her husband for about four months while working part-time at DBSC and continuing fieldwork. During that time, I was integrated into a group of friends and colleagues who were routinely exposed to these practices. As a result, we no longer froze on contact, and, without necessarily noticing, our boundaries around touch had been revised. For example, when Adrijana and I would go out together, she would often start the encounter by touching my feet, feeling the type and texture of shoes I was wearing. She would feel for the style of pants at the ankle and then trace the fabric up the shin to the knee. From there, she would skip to the belt and feel for the thickness and the texture. Then she would move to the neckline of the shirt and do a quick scan of the sleeves before feeling the style and state of the hair—Still wet? Ponytail? Straightened? Curly? All the while, she would be pulling in gulps of air through her nose, clearly gathering olfactory details as well. Finally, I would add any information that she wasn't likely to discover; for example, if we were wearing the same color, I might mention that. We usually disagreed about something. Adrijana thought our shoes were the same, and I didn't. Or she would (in good humor) accuse me of stealing her style, and I would try to defend myself. These arguments often ended with her telling me to feel rather than look at the item under dispute and once I had done that, I would often concede. Visually there were differences, but through touch the similarities stood out instead.

Although we were close friends and roommates, this kind of thing felt no more intimate than a friend commenting on your clothes when they see you: "I like your shirt." Or: "Look! We're matching!" Outside of our small group of friends, however, it was clearly counter to the norm. In the broader community, people were still suspended in mid-air and lacking particularity. Attempts to fill in the details were continually thwarted. When Adrijana became the director of DBSC, the staff there was no exception:

> Everyone was like that. Especially Deaf employees. If you came up and put your hands on them, they would either freeze or say "Hold on, I'm talking to someone." Or, "I'll be done in a sec."

In the past, Adrijana couldn't always prevent this sort of response, but now that she was the director of DBSC changes like this were within the scope of her job responsibilities. It wasn't just for her. She wanted DeafBlind people to have a sense of ownership and belonging in this organization that was established specifically for them.

4.2 "The Family Was Almost Dead"

Sitting in her office at DBSC, walking around the halls, entering into the conference room, Adrijana was struck, first and foremost, by the silence and utter lack of feeling. As Adrijana put it:

> The family was almost dead. It was like the Adams family. No character, no spirit, no nothing. It was just a vacant, bureaucratic feeling.

For the sighted people who worked there, Adrijana's sense of DBSC as lifeless and vacant might have seemed odd or unexpected. However, when sensory orientation shifts slowly, as it had over the years for Adrijana, what counts as self-evident shifts with it.

For example, in the summer of 2006, I did a lot of people-watching with Helen. We went to places like the farmer's market, restaurants, the dog park, and I passed along "snap-shots" of what I saw, adjusting the focus of description as instructed. On one of these excursions, we were wandering around in Seattle's Capitol Hill neighborhood, and we stumbled into an art opening. The following is taken from my field notes written afterward:

> I started with the hammers. Helen said not to bother, she wanted the feet. So we found a corner and started with the feet, which required attention to the legs.

"The toe is planted and the heel is swiveling right to left and back again" I say.

"I don't understand, show me," Helen says.

So I plant my toes and swivel my right foot. Helen pats down my leg, while I continue. She makes it down to the toes and back up again, and then says she gets it. She imitates me and asks if that's it. I confirm.

"Woman or man?" she asks.

"Woman."

"Is she talking to a woman or a man?"

"Man."

"Next."

It turns out that that woman was not the only woman talking to a man and swiveling one of her feet back and forth, pivoting on the toes. There were others. Helen notes that when a woman flirts, she is likely to engage in this particular movement of the foot. I move to the right. Two men are next to a very large sculpture of gears. They are facing each other, feet anchored:

"They're not moving their feet at all?" Helen asks.

"Nope."

"Men or women?"

"Men."

"What about the rest of their bodies? What are they doing?"

"Their hands are in their pockets, their heads are nodding, almost imperceptibly, and they're looking at the floor. Every once in a while, they look at each other and then quickly back to the floor," I say.

"They're looking at the floor and their hands are in their pockets?" Helen asks.

"Yep."

As we made our way around the room, it became clear that these men were not the only ones with their hands in their pockets. There were others. In fact this was almost an entirely generalizable feature of the room. It was a room in which hands were pocketed:

"Feet anchored, eyes averted, hands in pockets."

"Left foot anchored, right foot swiveling, hands in pockets."

And it goes on like this, until Helen becomes concerned. She says, "What are they doing with their hands in their pockets? Isn't this a party?" She hadn't remembered that hearing people stand around with their hands in their pockets, since they've got their mouths and their eyes for talking and seeing and such. She said she must have known that before she was blind. We went over the room again, scouring for hands caught mid-activity, and there were almost no cases to report. She accused them of being devoid of feeling. She accused them of being cold. But after thinking about it longer, she said, "Those poor people! They have too many limbs! They don't know what to do with them!"

For me, the pocketed hands, the averted eyes, and the swiveling feet all faded into the background as expectable features of an awkward social event. Helen, on the other hand, had been relying on interpreters to read social scenes for years. Slowly, their descriptions diverged from her direct encounters with the world.

When interpreters used words and phrases like "party" and "art opening," as I did, those words were meant to refer to a setting with particular characteristics. For me, these words conjured certain kinds of people, behaviors, objects, and activities. Meanwhile, Helen's environment was shifting beneath the words. While interpreters went on describing objects, scenes, and encounters in a way that conjured the environment as they experienced it, she was filling in the details in ways they couldn't have imagined. Insofar as high-level descriptions like "party" stood alone, no conflict arose. However, when the description operated a few notches down, to include more specific and concrete details, connections between the world and the descriptions of the world became glaringly problematic.

This gap between being in and talking about a place is an effect of the social, political, and historical paths taken by the Seattle DeafBlind community in the decades prior. When the community began to grow in the 1980s, the response was not to seek out affordances in the environment for direct, tactile communication, but rather to establish a DeafBlind identity, on the basis of which resources could be obtained from state government to pay for sighted interpreters (Chapter 2). In other words, the community started not with *affordances*, but with *identity*.

In the framework developed in this book, "affordance" and "identity" are located on opposite ends of a uni-directional process (Chapter 3). This is the idea: The world contains instruments, which we grasp in terms of their affordances for action. In performing actions habitually, we take on roles, and in routinely taking on roles, we have an identity. Represented schematically:

affordance → instrument → action → role → identity.

This process yields a way of *residing* in the world and is distinct from but related to ways of *representing* the world. While "the representational whole" has constituents of its own (Kockelman 2006b: 76), coherence between the two is presumed such that each is a really just a different "slice" of the same thing (Kockelman 2006a: 20). This coherence did not hold for Helen and me because at that point, the Seattle DeafBlind community was proceeding backwards through the constituents of the residential whole. As a result, there was no shared way of interpreting affordances in the environment, and without that, the most ordinary scenes became shocking, alarming, and confounding.

For example, in an interview, Lee explained that sighted people living in Seattle are familiar with downtown hotels. They expect to find automatic, sliding glass doors at the entrance. They anticipate the slightly squishy floor mat as they pass through the threshold. If they are holding a paper coffee cup, only a half-glance will be necessary to confirm the existence of a cylindrical silver trash can into which they can dispose of their cup. "It's always the same!" Lee said. However, she explained that DeafBlind people have, until recently, relied on sighted interpreters to navigate public spaces, preventing them from tracking those connections. As a result, Lee says, scenes like the following are likely to unfold:

> A DeafBlind person walks into a [hotel], and runs into the garbage can turning the corner. They look shocked and tell the person they're with that the placement of the trash can is not safe!

Outbursts like this strike others as unwarranted, since from a sighted perspective, the placement of the trash can is expectable. Lee pointed out that a DeafBlind person using a cane and paying attention to their surroundings without passing through someone else's visual perspective would notice regularities like this as well. But they didn't, and this made it seem like they were out of touch with reality.

I lived in Seattle and was involved in the DeafBlind community as an interpreter and in other capacities for seven years before I went to graduate school. During that time, I had witnessed many events like the one Lee described. For example, one day, I entered a coffee shop with a DeafBlind man. I told him there were several people in line ahead of us. He responded by repeatedly adjusting his footing, saying "Sorry. Sorry." He clenched his fists and cringed, as if bracing for a collision. Or I would say something banal about what I was looking at, and they would yell, "I'm sorry!" "I didn't know!" or "I'm blind!" These events always seemed quirky to me. However, looking back now, I see them as signs that ASL had too many demands placed on it, and its capacity to convey even the most basic facts about the environment was breaking down.

The statement, "There are several people in line ahead of us," could mean many things. It could mean, "You just cut in line. You're being rude." It could mean, "This looks like it's going to take no time at all." Or it could mean, "It looks like we might be here a while." Each one of these interpretations would be reasonable under different circumstances, insofar as those circumstances were self-evident to *us*. At the time, though, unexpected responses to information like those I described above accrued to individual DeafBlind people (not their relation to the environment). They were "odd" or "eccentric." People would sometimes recall the way they "used to be" and wonder aloud about their "decline." At some level, then, these problems were being attributed to the failures of the individual.

In the years leading up to those exchanges, efforts to carve out a space for DeafBlind people started with established socio-political structures. Within those structures, a legible identity was established, and on that basis, state and local resources were tapped. However, operating within those structures tended to reinforce what was appropriate for sighted people, not what was effective for DeafBlind people, and being in the world became increasingly abstract (Chapter 3). Leaders of the protactile movement went a different way. Instead of finding ways to approximate sighted experiences, or access sighted environments, they started instead by relinquishing attachments to visual ways of being in the world, and relaxing normative constraints on touch.

The staff at DBSC included three tactile DeafBlind people: Adrijana, Jodi, and Lee. Having three tactile DeafBlind staff members was unprecedented and there were no communication conventions in place for three-way tactile communication. In the past, if there were more than two DeafBlind people present, interpreters would be hired to mediate. In an interview in 2010, Adrijana explained:

> If Jodi and I were talking and Lee wanted to join, we had to figure that out. It wasn't obvious to us at first, but we tried to follow our intuitions and find a way to communicate between the three of us. [...] We weren't really reflective about it. We just kind of did what worked, which was signing with two hands. Then when sighted people would join us, they would look confused—like how am I supposed to communicate with both of you at once? And we would tell them to sign with two hands. We didn't do that if we had to have a meeting for an hour. We did that for short meetings—10 minutes here, 10 minutes there. I didn't want to explain things to one staff person, and then repeat myself with the second person. That would eat up too much time. So it was a good way of efficiently conveying a short message.

When Adrijana says "signing with two hands," she is talking about an innovative way of *using* the two hands that differed from the way they are used in ASL. In ASL, the dominant hand of the signer produces certain aspects of a signed expression, while the non-dominant hand is there in a "support" role. In the interactions Adrijana described, both hands were playing the role of the dominant hand (see Edwards 2014: 192–222 for a detailed analysis of this phenomenon).

These practices quickly became naturalized among the staff at DBSC. So much so, that they were surprised when others found them novel:

> It became so normal for me in such a short period of time that I didn't think about it. But when people saw it, they would respond—like "Wow! That's so cool!" And I remember saying, "Well, they do that at the Lighthouse, too," and being told that they didn't do anything like that there. That was a big insight for me […]. I didn't even realize that that was the case until about a year later. I didn't come to the realization that there was a discrepancy in how communication was happening inside DBSC and outside. It had all happened so naturally that we didn't think about each little thing we did. No one really talked about it much. It was just an ongoing negotiation and people were expected to do what it took to make themselves understood and understand other people.

From 2006 to 2007, communication within DBSC was already moving away from reliance on interpreters and toward direct communication between DeafBlind people. Conventions for communicating with sighted people that included more tactile practices were also emerging. This shift eased financial and scheduling strains. DBSC had very limited funds and interpreters were expensive. The scheduling process itself was time consuming as well, and in order to get the right interpreters they had to be booked far in advance. All of those problems grew more severe as the interpreter shortage worsened.

As Adrijana explained, there were often situations where an impromptu meeting was needed that required the presence of more than one DeafBlind staff member and using interpreters was not feasible. In addition, Adrijana noted that people didn't want to include DeafBlind people in their organizations or events because paying for interpreters for them was so expensive. Therefore, she said, "changing our communication practices could help solve that problem in addition to the day-to-day logistical problem of wanting to have short, spontaneous meetings."

When internal dynamics started changing for the better, there was friction with people from outside the organization who came to DBSC regularly and hadn't been privy to the changes. That friction, Adrijana said, "made the staff more insistent and gave them the inspiration to get serious about establishing a DeafBlind friendly zone." A certain repertoire of DeafBlind friendly communicative practices had become naturalized within DBSC, and their naturalization made it difficult to describe them explicitly. As Adrijana says below, even if outsiders wanted to learn (which was not often the case in the beginning), naturalization was a barrier to teaching them:

> At first, I thought that communicating in a DeafBlind friendly way was common sensical, or at least easy to learn. But I realized that people don't like change. These were all big insights for me and I realized that I had to be more patient, take things in baby steps, approach people more gently. We had to ask people nicely. We didn't want to post big threatening signs [...], so I decided we would just have to go with the flow more, and be patient about change. That process took about two years—from 2006 to 2008.

By the end of 2008, the internal dynamics of DBSC were greatly improved and efforts turned to increasing the relevance and quality of services. The goal was to bring the internal culture of DBSC out into the community and re-evaluate problems on that basis.

4.3 When the Problem Is the Solution

DBSC contracts with state agencies, such as the Department of Services for the Blind to provide specialized, direct services to DeafBlind people. Therefore, what counts as a legitimate service is shaped as much by the structures and categories of the state agencies as it is by the needs and desires of the community. Adrijana had to find ways of addressing the discrepancies:

> We noticed, as staff at DBSC, that senior citizens were coming in droves to discuss problems they were having. When we looked at what was going on, there usually wasn't a problem. It seemed like they were home alone, socially isolated, going crazy, and had to invent a reason to come in and talk to someone. And then they would have to get caught up in some kind of imaginary problem as their only form of socializing. The advocate would get overwhelmed with all of this work that wasn't really legitimate. They needed to have some kind of positive interaction. The goal was to relieve some of the problems that seemed to come from being isolated–paranoia, stress, etc.—and it worked.

Given the fact that severe social isolation was a real problem for older DeafBlind people, it seemed like they would have gotten together more often on their own. There were two main reasons they didn't. First, even if they had, they wouldn't be able to communicate with one another in groups, since no conventions had been established for this. Second, there was what Adrijana called a "leadership" problem:

> A lot of people were retiring, so what were they going to do? That problem became a first priority. We asked the senior citizens to bring their own SSPs rather than DBSC being responsible for coordinating SSPs, and each month they would be responsible for planning an event themselves. We called that "leadership," and we expected it to go alright. But then we found out that they weren't doing anything. They weren't finding their own SSPs, they weren't planning their own events. It was really surprising. They had just gotten so used to someone else doing everything for them. They'll find me an SSP, they'll plan the events, and so on. Conversations often went like this:
>
> **DEAFBLIND SENIOR CITIZEN:** I need a ride.
> **DBSC STAFF PERSON:** You find your own ride! Use the bus! Or call a cab!
>
> And then nothing happened. So that was an indication of what had been going on all this time—people had become complacent and unable to do things for themselves, or at least not used to doing things for themselves. So I got really frustrated, and they got irritated, being asked to do things they didn't want to do and weren't accustomed to doing. So my great idea didn't work, because people didn't just snap into the role that I had in mind. I had to try to do what they expected, rather than trying to make them the kind of DeafBlind people I thought they should be. So I hired a coordinator for the DeafBlind Senior Citizen program. The goal then, was for that person to figure out how to work with DeafBlind people to build leadership potential without making the mistakes I had made, moving too fast and expecting things to change too quickly.

Essentially, Adrijana was asking people who had spent many years in the role of "the served" to step into the role of the service provider. Theresa Smith, a long time ethnographer in the Seattle DeafBlind community, writes about the problems this division between those who provide and those who receive services has caused (2002):

> Agencies naturally take their direction from the people who establish, fund and run them. Agencies serving DeafBlind people are typically funded and run by people outside the community. [...] [Therefore] the people in positions of power and authority come from a different world than the people for whom the agency is established. This is a problem. Hearing/Sighted administrators and staff do not

share the life experience (deafness, blindness) or socio-economic class (income and life style) of their clients. They do not even share a primary language and culture. Few professionals on staff and fewer administrators have native-like fluency in ASL and Deaf culture [...]. This creates an almost insurmountable gap in world view and in access to power. This difference in power has been institutionalized. [...] We want to move beyond the limits of the present to a future in which Deaf-Blind people have not only power but authority and control within these agencies established in their name.

Although there is a great deal of variation among DeafBlind people in terms of socio-economic class, life experience, access to education, etc., the roles of those providing and receiving services have historically been opposed and mutually exclusive. Therefore, if someone was receiving services, they were by definition not making decisions about how those services were administered.

This led to problems like those that the senior citizens were experiencing. There was no agency contracting with DBSC to pay for social events as a way of alleviating social isolation. DeafBlind people knew this, so they had to make their attempts at socializing into a problem suitable for the services that were provided. One of the unfortunate side effects was that DeafBlind senior citizens were shaped by the negative and irrelevant role they were often left playing. They had to put on a performance of distress sufficient to justify a meeting with the advocate. Although they were experiencing distress, the nature and cause of the distress had to be disguised in order to alleviate it.

For DBSC's staff, redirecting some funds and organizing social events was much preferable to sifting through the details of intentionally confusing stories, as well as being overwhelmed by the number of clients who came in telling them. Furthermore, Adrijana thought DeafBlind people shouldn't have to be in crisis in order to have human contact. The order of operations should be just the opposite. They should have human contact in order to avoid crisis. Therefore, she decided to use part of the advocacy budget to pay for minimal support to a DeafBlind Senior Citizen's program. However, one meeting of the group required many volunteer interpreters (about two per participant). Soon after its inception, then, interpreters became a problem.

4.4 Learning about the World

Louise, a DeafBlind senior, and the first volunteer coordinator of the DeafBlind seniors program, described her attempts to keep the program up and running:

Now we have a new director at DBSC, Adrijana, who asked me to work with the senior citizen's program, trying to get it back on its feet, which I agreed to do. I have found volunteer [interpreters] who are ASL students. The students who have been helping have been absolutely wonderful. Right now we have 10 senior citizens in the program who are very happy to have the program back. But it is uncertain what will happen in the fall because many of our volunteers have to go to school. Some will find jobs. We need funding to pay for [. . .] [interpreters]. We want to get out of the house and learn more about the world. Many of us stay home for long periods of time, and are very lonely. Just yesterday I got a call from one senior citizen, who was crying because she was so lonely. She just wanted to get out of her house, but there were no [interpreters] available. It's really bad.

The shortage of interpreters was the problem on the surface of things, but if interpreters weren't used, there would no longer be a problem. This, however, would require a major transition where DeafBlind people learned to communicate directly with one another. If this could be accomplished, social isolation could be addressed without appealing to sighted people for support, and further taxing the already depleted interpreting resources.

Once Adrijana took up her post as director of DBSC, she and her new staff found that many of the problems they hoped to address, when thought through, were linked to the absence of direct contact with other people and the world. Why, for example, would a DeafBlind person need an interpreter or "SSP" to "learn more about the world"? One reason, Adrijana said, was that many DeafBlind people didn't possess the technical skill of tactile reception. She and her team wanted to make learning that skill appealing. They thought it was strange that in the past, sighted people had often been the ones to teach tactile skills to DeafBlind people, even though they didn't use that form of communication themselves. They thought that DeafBlind people should be the ones to teach it—not only because it was more practical, as they were the ones who really knew how it worked, but also because DeafBlind people should be able to turn this practical knowledge into expertise as such, which they could not do without opportunities to teach.

All of this went into planning a series of classes, which would be offered by DBSC to DeafBlind people, and taught by DeafBlind people, without the use of interpreters. The problem was that if they advertised the class as having anything to do with going tactile, no one would sign up—and especially not the ones who in Adrijana and Lee's view really needed to sign up. Adrijana explained that "we knew the word 'tactile' would turn them off, so we changed it to 'DeafBlind to DeafBlind class.' That piqued people's curiosity, because they didn't already know what it was." Most of the classes did not thematize tactility. They were about finance, cooking, wood-working, and other topics. The instructors, though, were all DeafBlind, as were the students, and no interpreters were provided. Tunnel-vision and tactile people were thrown together and expected to communicate directly with one another.

People who had not yet gone tactile were encouraged to wear blindfolds, but not required to do so. Lee taught the classes, and one of her main strategies was to have discussion groups. She organized people into pairs sitting opposite one another, and then gave them a question to discuss. After 5–7 minutes, she had them rotate so that every person in the room discussed the question with every other person in the room. It seemed time consuming, but she naturalized the process for the participants by saying "this is our culture" and "this is how we do things." This way of doing things had benefits that she didn't state explicitly in the classes but that, she told me later, shaped her approach:

> It meant that there was more equality in access to information. When a group of sighted people are in a room together, they can all be looking at one another. Everyone knows what everyone thinks, what everyone feels, and what everyone says [...]. It doesn't work to get everything through one person [an interpreter]. Then you're totally disconnected from your environment and the people in it. I was interested in finding a way to make group engagement possible—such that you would feel actually connected to the people you were with and the place you were in.

At this early stage in the protactile movement, Lee was asking people to let go of who they were as tactile or tunnel-vision people (i.e. their *identities*), and focus instead on interpreting affordances in new ways that could correspond across the group. Starting with affordances and allowing one's ideas about what constituted things like "group engagement" to shift to accommodate affordances made new forms of action possible.

4.5 Motivating Action

When I asked Adrijana about those early protactile workshops, she said they didn't feel like an extraordinary success. The reason, she explained had to do with two, interconnected facts: First, as we see in Lee's encounters, people had identities, which they did not just relinquish on request. Second, those identities were bound up with certain prescriptions for how information should flow. Adrijana explained:

> People already have their ways of doing things. Senior Citizens love to go to the monthly meetings [at DBSC] in order to talk to their [interpreters]! They love it because they get information from them. They don't see DeafBlind people as a source of information....

Information flowed from sighted people to DeafBlind people and this pattern had institutional roots. As individuals became blind, they generally had less opportunity to occupy the role of the "service provider" and were increasingly thrust into the role of the "served" (Smith 2002). Where information was concerned, that role meant being a recipient of information, maybe a relay for information, but never its primary source.

When Adrijana explained that DeafBlind people were not seen as a source of information, she left room for the possibility that this was a bias people had but maybe not representative of the facts as she experienced them, so I asked her if she thought it was true that DeafBlind people didn't have any information to share. She said:

> I think DeafBlind people have a disconnect between information that they have and ways of expressing it. I think when interpreters share information, it gets their minds working again—connections start happening, and then they can share with other DeafBlind people. It's like their brains come alive again, but they need a kick start.

This "disconnect" does not derive merely from lack of contact with others. It runs deeper, since whatever information, knowledge, or experience that is generated in daily life is generated primarily via tactile channels. Prior to the protactile movement, the way the environment was channeled differed across individuals, even if all of the individuals involved were "tactile" people. There was no shared, tactile world. To make matters more complicated, there was no system of representation available for expressing knowledge about any tactile world, shared or not. Therefore, while individuals may have been exploring in their own way, accruing idiosyncratic forms of knowledge, there was, in Adrijana's terms, a disconnect between the information they had and the means they had for expressing it.

In the years leading up to this moment, interventions were based on the widespread assumption that if connections between DeafBlind people and the world were growing tenuous, sighted people could be inserted as a relay, and the whole world would be kept intact (Chapter 2). However, Adrijana is pointing here to widespread problems that arose as this relay system played out over time. Most fundamentally, DeafBlind people were drifting away into their own idiosyncratic world. At some level, communication was still possible. Utterances, more or less, made their way from one DeafBlind person to another, but the utility, relevance, and impact of those utterances were compromised since the receiver had no way to tell if the effects of utterances and other signs on *them* corresponded in any way to the effects they had on *others*. This applied just as much to complex acts of communication as it did to basic interactions with the environment.

In a shared world, we observe the refraction of events of all kinds across participants. Our attention is drawn, as children, to differences in how individuals and types of individuals respond in more or less effective and appropriate ways to conflict, accident, injury, and so on. As we develop into adulthood, we internalize some behaviors and not others as the "right" way, or the "wrong" way to respond, and our sensibilities about the kinds of people we like, respect, or dismiss begin to form. By virtue of that process, we find ourselves repulsed by, drawn to, or unaffected by certain people, and we can feel others' indifference, attraction, or repulsion to us. Even inanimate things call out to us, or repel us, in particular ways (Clark 2015; Gibson 2015 [1977]). Being caught up on those dynamics is part of what it means to be someone (in particular). In other words, action *in* the world presupposes being affected *by* the world.

Adrijana, in recalling the earliest protactile workshops, homed in on these dynamics, and their absence, among tactile people. She explained that things went along alright as long as the workshops were being led by a tunnel-vision person, but then there was a class taught by Robert, a tactile person. Adrijana said, "Everyone assumed since Robert was a blind DeafBlind person, that he would be with an interpreter. But just like all of the other classes, no one had an interpreter. Several students dropped the class when they found that out. Robert felt demoralized." I asked Adrijana if people gave a reason when they dropped the class and she said they had: "There are no interpreters and Robert is blind." It turns out that when pressed further, they didn't feel safe. Robert was teaching wood-working and he was using a large, electric saw and a drill. Adrijana explains:

> Before Robert even plugged in the machine, they were scared to death. Robert just wanted to show them the machine and they freaked out. They thought there would be interpreters there, and they would have more of an observational role, but that isn't what we had in mind.

I asked Adrijana if she thought their fears were warranted, and she said that at first she didn't think so. But then a while later, she was helping make a bunch of cloth napkins for a DeafBlind event with friends—both DeafBlind and sighted—all of whom had significantly more vision than she did. She fearlessly ventured forth with the sewing machine and ended up putting the needle through her index finger. "I laughed," she said, "but it hurt like hell." After that, she changed her perspective on the issue.

People didn't trust their ability to interpret tactile signals in their environment, and they didn't trust that people would be able to communicate about the environment in ways that would prevent injury when trying to use a dangerous machine. They were right. Not only were their sensory orientations always shifting, there was a definite disconnect between tactile experience and the visual language they had at their disposal, ASL. In addition, there was a great deal of variation among the group in terms of sensory orientation and there were no conventionalized practices that established meaningful correspondences across those differences. All of this made learning how to use new, potentially dangerous equipment without the use of interpreters a bad idea. In a shared world, representations of the world and the world itself are intricately interwoven in childhood and into adulthood. We internalize those connections and on that basis we build instruments (such as sewing machines, cars, and microscopes). We interact with the world based not only on the relation between our bodies, the environment, and the affordances therein, but also on the basis of how others have done so before us, the pathways they have built for us, and the tools they have created.

Leaders of the protactile movement intuitively grasped these complexities and they took a very different path than the one taken in the decades prior. Instead of trying to maintain pre-existing norms, they shifted attention to latent affordances in the environment that could speak, in corresponding ways, across the collective. Without this, there was little motivation to speak, interact with others, or interact with the environment, and in fact there were real deterrents to doing so.

4.6 Re-defining Roles

As action was motivated, the roles available to DeafBlind people in Seattle, and the value associated with those roles, began to shift. The process, however, was not seamless. For example, Adrijana told me that in the 2007 protactile workshops, people kept dropping the class—a first round dropped the class because they didn't trust that blind people could operate instruments designed by sighted people, and they didn't see blind people as information-sources in the first place. The next round of people who dropped the course, according to Adrijana, did so when they were asked to go to a coffee shop and use tactile communication in public. While many of them were willing to communicate through touch in a private class, they were unwilling to do so in public. Each of these exit points in the 2007 workshops revealed something about roles and the value associated with them. And then there was the question of language.

I asked Adrijana, in 2010, if she thought that there had been an effect on language and communication practices, despite the initial lack of enthusiasm about the classes and the difficulty they had trying to keep people from leaving. Her response went back to the resiliency (or not) of roles:

> What I think has been happening is that there is more overlap. Before there was a crystal clear separation between [tunnel-vision people] and [tactile people]. Now they are mixing a little.

She went on to explain that homogenization of communication practices seemed necessary and also posed a serious challenge, as those practices were rooted in particular roles and, importantly, asymmetric role-relations:

> There's so much variation. Now we're just trying to slowly close the gap between the two sides. That will help people to transition to our side—the tactile side—and it will keep people from being able to reject us. They can't do that any more. So my experience of the changes since 2007 really includes this narrowing of the gap and a recognition of the importance of that. All this time I thought that it really hadn't gotten any better and that was that. But deep down, I knew we had gotten off to a great start. It's just that I had no idea how it would grow or if it would. That's why I say it's all very new, and things are changing very slowly. As far as how it will all end up, I think we have to wait five years or something to find out.

Over the next decade, a major shift in roles had transpired. At the time Adrijana is recounting, the tactile/tunnel-vision divide was robust, and for reasons discussed in previous chapters, there was a clear preference for tunnel-vision status. Since then, the relevant distinction has become "protactile" vs. "not protactile." Being protactile means greater access to status, employment, and opportunities of all kinds (Edwards 2018). In addition, communication practices, as well as the linguistic system itself, have changed radically (Clark and Nuccio 2020; Edwards and Brentari 2020).

At the time, though, Adrijana was far from certain that roles were changing and she wasn't sure if anything at all in the language itself had changed. She said that she thought some things were new—like describing spatial relations by pointing to locations on the palm of the addressee rather than in the space in front of the signer, but she said that, "in DeafBlind to DeafBlind class we never talked about it. We just did what we did. I don't even know what we did. Really, you're asking me if things have changed and I don't really know." If things had changed, it wasn't clear when certain practices had come into use, or how widely they were in use. She was certain that they didn't teach any new communication practices in these first classes. People "just started picking things up from other people and incorporating what [they] liked. And then some of it stuck and was history."

4.7 Going Tactile

As I started my dissertation research in 2010, Adrijana and Lee were looking for another opportunity to teach classes like the ones they had taught before in 2007, but funding had been scarce, and they had been busy with other projects. I was looking for ways to systematically observe the changes in communication and language that had been occurring, so I contributed part of my dissertation funding for a second round of classes. We started having planning meetings in the fall of 2010 and the classes started that winter. Adrijana and Lee prepared the content of the courses and selected and recruited participants. I helped coordinate logistics and managed tasks specific to research, such as organizing the collection of video data and obtaining consent from participants. A team of sighted people videorecorded the classes, but did not otherwise take part in them. There were two groups: Group A and Group B—each comprised of five or six students and two teachers. Ten two-hour classes were offered to Group A over the course of five weeks and ten two-hour classes were offered to Group B, also over the course of five weeks.

When the participants arrived, they were told once again that they would have to figure out how to communicate with each other, without any interpreters. Adrijana already knew, from past experience, that getting rid of sighted mediators would be badly received, but Adrijana and Lee were persistent. They felt that what they were doing was natural, or intuitive, and once people started doing it, they would be hooked. By the time they started with the second group, Group B, they had some learning objectives, and some experience in achieving them. One of those learning objectives was to get people in the habit of sitting together in ways that made consistent, tactile contact, a given. This, they argued, would generate a basis for tactile interaction and communication. There are many ways this might have been accomplished, but during the first five weeks of the workshops, with Group A, they had settled on particular conventions.

Lee explained, for example, that in a group of three, people should have their knees touching and their legs pointing inward toward a common center, so each person could comfortably reach the thigh of the other two people. Her reasoning was as follows:

> I like always having three legs in contact with each other, here [touching Amanda's leg], here [touching her own leg] and here [touching George's leg]. If our legs are always in contact, then we don't have to go looking for each other, we just know that the other people are there, and how they are positioned in relation to us. You know, you don't want to accidentally reach out and touch the other person in a way you didn't mean, or in a way they didn't expect. When we sit like this, we're right here together and we can feel that and we can respond to things other people say.

It is clear here that Lee's first focus is on co-presence—"We are all here together." This particular way of sitting started to occur and became conventional during Group A's workshops. It happened, people noticed it was happening and drew attention to it, it was tested, and it worked, so Lee and Adrijana called it "protactile." Now, in this stretch of interaction, Lee is introducing this as an established practice, and is pointing out the benefits of it. She goes on to say:

> If Amanda is talking, George and I can move our hands to her leg like this [demonstrates], and tap on her leg to show we are listening and interested in what she is saying. Then when George starts talking, we can move our hands onto his leg, all together. Deaf people use their eyes for that. If a Deaf person wasn't maintaining eye contact when you were talking to them, you would say, "Hey! Pay attention!" Right? [both students nod, but do not provide tactile feedback]. DeafBlind people need that same thing—they need to establish attention—and they do that by putting their hands on each other's thighs, instead of maintaining eye contact. Being in contact like this, tapping, it's like saying, "I'm here, and I'm paying attention to you."

Lee's students immediately understand the relevance and importance of this. George, however, is poised for a set of rules. He wants to know what the technique is, exactly—Where exactly should you touch the other person, and how? What does each small difference mean? Lee answers that there are no specific rules, or rigid meanings. The point, she says, is to think about whether or not the other person can *feel* what you are doing and from there, you just "express yourself" by tapping or squeezing their leg, for example, just as a hearing person might nod or say "mmmmm," or gasp, so they know you're listening and how you feel.

Conventions like this were established, reflected on, named, and characterized as "protactile." This made it possible to interpret affordances in new ways, thereby motivating new pathways for action, which in turn, affected the reconfiguration of roles and the value that accrued to those roles. Ultimately, this process gave rise to a new "protactile" way of being DeafBlind, such that you could ask, "Is she protactile?" and there would be a clear answer to that question.

It all starts with particular ways of reading affordances in the environment in ways that correspond across the group. For example, the idea that changing the way you habitually sit with others for purposes of conversation so your legs can be in constant contact. Then, within that configuration, realizing together that different ways of tapping or squeezing might have affordances for backchanneling, or telling the person who is speaking that you are listening and how you feel about what they are saying. Uncovering affordances for co-presence, or just being together, leads to the discovery of additional affordances, and so on. Across those various domains, patterns in how affordances are interpreted begin to form, which are detectable across the group and can be extended to new domains. This is why, as opposed to interpreter-mediated interaction, protactile practices feel *intuitive*. This is a refrain from both Lee and Adrijana: *What we are doing here is intuitive*—not on the level of the individual, but for the collective. I express myself in a way that feels intuitive to me and that I anticipate will feel intuitive to you as well. If it doesn't, it falls out of the experiment. If it does, it gets picked up and is history.

Many practices were ratified and quickly internalized by Group A, including a habit of pulling the listener's hand to the signer's throat when laughing, so they could feel the particular vibration of the signer's laugh. Prior to this moment, DeafBlind people and interpreters told one another they were laughing by producing a manual sign, "Ha Ha," which is borrowed from English via fingerspelling. Someone would say something funny, and the listener would say, "H-A H-A." Now, Lee was introducing something different—something that had already been internalized by her and others, as "protactile" in Group A's session a few weeks earlier. Amanda, however, had only experienced this strange practice with a single individual—Roman. Roman was many things that Amanda was not. He was tall and Amanda was short. He had grown up mostly in hearing environments and she had grown up mostly in Deaf environments. He did whatever it took to communicate. She was concerned with decorum. So when Lee pulled the back of Amanda's hand to Lee's throat, Amanda said, "Like Roman! I hate it when he does that!"

Lee pauses for a moment to consider this potentially unfavorable association, but she says that Roman is just one person. "What if everyone does it?" she says, "Then it might come off differently." Amanda counters that Roman is too tall, so when he pulls your hand to his throat, your hand goes straight up in the air and then runs into his tall, weird throat. Lee again pauses to consider this unfortunate association and says, optimistically, that there are solutions to all of these things. Ken, she says, is another tall person, and what he does is bend over when he's communicating with short people. Then she laughs and pulls her hands to her throat so they can feel her laughing. It's funny—the image of big, tall Ken, lumbering over to small people and then hovering above them to communicate. They go on talking about really tall DeafBlind people they know and really short DeafBlind people they know trying to communicate and then they laugh, each time pulling the listeners' hands to the backs of their throats. George says: "Ken and Lynn! She's so short! Like this tall. . . ." He holds his hand, palm down, about 3 feet above the ground and laughs, pulling Lee and Amanda's hands to his throat as he doubles over and his face turns red. All three collapse into laughter together. Transcribing it, I laughed too. It's hilarious! Meanwhile, as they laugh, they pull one another's hands to their throats. This practice had caught on only a couple of minutes after it was introduced, even in the midst of protest against it.

Interactions like these support Adrijana and Lee's claims that protactile practices are so intuitive that they can go from new to part of the common sense in minutes, no matter what the explicit arguments against it may be. It's as if common pathways to the environment were already there— DeafBlind people just had to clear off the clutter that stood in the way and they would drop right in. When I say clutter, I mean negative associations people have with certain channels, modalities, and specific practices therein, such as Amanda's complaints above, and also normative constraints that apply more broadly. Several people complained when this hand-to-throat practice was introduced that it seemed like an "oral" thing. For them, all things "oral" were self-evidently bad so a negative value accrued to the practice. However, this practice was not about accessing speech or sound. It was about vibration: to tap the affordances of vibration and the very specific differences that could be detected in each person's laughter. Deaf sighted norms had to be pushed aside.

Another time, early on in the second set of workshops, Lee was teaching a student how to give simple feedback on the leg of the speaker, by tapping. The student said, "OK, I see how this works when you're sitting down, but what about when you're standing up?" Lee responds by saying, "I've been talking to

Adrijana about this, but you know what's great about all of this. When you're standing up with other people, suddenly you realize you already know what to do." There is a sense that, even if you can't explain how something will work, as you become more protactile you will just know what to do. It is a matter of reinforcing your own intuitions or paying attention to what you already understand about the world, often without realizing. Being protactile begins in collective interpretations of affordances, but in order for patterns of interpretation to converge, the possibility of convergence had to be taken for granted. This is not possible if the environment is hidden, out of bounds, or inconsistent.

For example, early on in Group B's workshops, one of the participants notices that she and another person in her group have this habit of holding their hands (which are in contact with the signer) up in the air while they are listening with their other hands to Lee. Their hands are up by their ears, hanging there in a really uncomfortable position. Lee tries to explain to them by saying that when their hands are up there they are disconnected from her as the speaker. Those hands are supposed to be providing feedback, and when they're not on her leg she can't tell if they're listening or not. Every time their hands float up, off of her leg, she pushes them back down. She does that repeatedly, but their hands keep floating back up. At some point, they all start laughing at how ridiculous this is. Their shoulders are getting sore, they're getting tired, and yet, they keep doing it. They can't explain their own behavior and in a protactile environment this habit suddenly seems absurd. Lee responds by saying:

> These problems of signing up here, and holding your hands up in this space, are all because of tunnel-vision. If you're used to signing for tunnel vision people, you're going to keep your hands up in that space where tunnel-vision people can see, as a habit. Even if a tunnel-vision person is talking to someone who is sighted, they sign like that because that's their signing space. [To the more tunnel-vision student:] It is something people like you and [another tunnel-vision person] do, and others who are not tactile. It's something you all do because you're used to communicating in that tunnel-vision way. Once you start communicating with tactile people, your arms come down, and can rest and be natural. It's really incredible how the body can change, slowly, and adapt to your experiences.

Lee is focused here not on how much vision a person has but on the channels that organize the person's environment and social network. We see in interactions like those recounted above that bridging the gap between tunnel-vision people and tactile people promises a form of stability required for "autonomous" interaction with the environment. To act in the world, the world must be there. This includes people too, so when you walk out your front door in the morning, you don't have to worry about limbs floating off or freezing in mid-air. You know, in some basic sense, how the ground will resist you when you step on it, what would happen if you jumped into a body of water, and how a person will be present to you when sharing the same physical space. Without assurances such as these, autonomous action in the world is impossible.

Lee and Adrijana worked against powerful forces to bring people into a common center. As they did that, the environment started sending out messages, which could be interpreted and acted on without hesitation. From there, many things became possible that had previously been impossible. For example, watching other people do things like knit a scarf, read a Braille book, or play a game. One of the games people played, and enjoyed watching, was called "Tactile Pictionary." Two people would sit facing each other, and they would take turns molding playdough into different shapes and then guessing what it was supposed to be. The observers would stand behind them, chest to back, hands on hands, tracking their movement. Afterward, the players reflected on the experience. They said: You know that playdough is being rolled out, but beyond that, you know how it is being rolled out—at what pace, with what intensity, and to what effect. From there, you can speculate about the temperament of the roller, or you can notice traces of their culinary habits mixed with the smell of their dog and their body and you can associate that unique olfactory combination with them like a fingerprint or a signature that can be recognized anywhere. You know that there is another person there, but beyond that you have access to the tension in the tendons and muscles of their hands, arms, and neck. From there you can speculate about their level of interest in the game or you can begin to appreciate their tactile agility as their fingers dart around the curves and corners of the sculpture, and then leap up off of the object to announce a best guess to the group. After a while, you begin to like people, or not. You begin to feel drawn into things, or repulsed by them. The meanings of utterances become overdetermined and expectable, and you begin to feel that you are part of a world.

Prior to the protactile movement, "going tactile" was something people did reluctantly and only when they could no longer operate in the tunnel-vision role. It did not lead to an intense and particular world that called forth action, since the only thing that really changed was the channel through which linguistic signs were transferred. The world itself was the world of the sighted. Going tactile meant that the distance between the self and the world was growing. In Chapter 3, I showed how the Seattle DeafBlind community, in the decades prior, addressed that growing distance by relying more on sighted interpreters to mediate. The first step toward mediation was establishing an identity, on the basis of which, resources are made available. The DeafBlind identities that process gave rise to were, however, resting on unstable ground. The reason, I argued, had to do with the order in which the world was reassembled. The world contains instruments, which we grasp in terms of their affordances for action. In performing actions habitually, we take on roles; and in routinely taking on roles, we have an identity, or way of being in the world (Kockelman 2006a). For the first three decades of Seattle's DeafBlind history, the community proceeded from identity to roles to action. Since the inception of the protactile movement, the community has begun to reverse this process. First, normative constraints and other clutter that kept tactile affordances hidden were removed and tactile affordances in the environment were seized upon. This motivated action and generated new roles, which gave rise to a new way of being DeafBlind.

This process increased "autonomy" (granda and Nuccio 2018). In observing the use of this term across interactions, however, it is clear that it does not map perfectly onto its English counterpart. The protactile word is produced by pressing the back of the fingers onto the center of the addressee's chest, while moving it down two times in rapid succession. Contact is made, more specifically, in a location associated with the heart. The resulting word combines a meaning derived from the ASL sign "inside" with the notion of "feeling" or "sense," derived from the location on the addressee's body where the word is produced. When the term is translated into English, it tends to be glossed "autonomy," but in use, it also aligns with notions of "intuition" and "effectiveness." A DeafBlind person is acting autonomously if they are seeking out affordances in their environment, which are intuitive and effective for them, rather than adhering to norms that are appropriate, but not effective. The protactile word asks people to direct their attention to tactile affordances in the environment, which are already present, but may be obscured. Once you are grasping affordances in the world rather than receiving descriptions of the world, new possibilities for who you can talk to, where you can go, and what you can do proliferate. You are less dependent on sighted guides and interpreters because the environment becomes interpretable, and therefore you have increased "autonomy" in the sense of the English word.

Depending on the complex set of identities DeafBlind persons might have, however, transgressions of dominant norms will present different kinds of consequences. For example, in 2020, Najma Johnson published an essay describing a conflict that, among white protactile leaders and theorists, had not been sufficiently addressed. Johnson writes:

> I truly love LOVE Protactile. It makes me feel great. There are some aspects of PT that do not sit well with me.... I love the concept/belief about autonomy behind PT. It is a wonderful thing for us to have autonomy AND it is not always realistic. Does [a DeafBlind person of color] have autonomy? No, not the same way as White DeafBlind folks. We could try and claim our autonomy. Unfortunately, it is regulated by White [DeafBlind people]. Race and Culture play a huge role with 'autonomy'.... It is IMPERATIVE that we require cultural flexibility.... Autonomy is not always positive for many of us.

Johnson points out that the risks for DeafBlind persons of color in breaking White norms are higher than for those who are White. Strain is felt unevenly and this is an ongoing point of tension as the protactile movement continues to grow and spread. Related issues have been raised by those who have experienced trauma associated with touch. In sighted societies, touch is severely restricted in terms of the functions it can serve (Clark 2017). Those functions are often limited to intimate encounters, violence, and child rearing. Therefore, when an individual has suffered trauma, the frequent touching experienced in protactile environments can be particularly hard to habituate to. In one case, for example, a young woman was interested in learning protactile, but disclosed to several of us that she had suffered abuse. The DeafBlind instructors leading the event worked out a step-wise plan to restrict touch and then slowly introduce new practices. I have observed variable success with approaches like these, and conversations are ongoing. A third and related problem involves DeafBlind people who have not had access to touch are therefore sometimes overwhelmed when there is a sudden stream of tactile stimuli to parse and interpret. All of these experiences generate different, and sometimes conflicting, points of entry into the project of building a more tactile world, and are points of tension at the center of public debate as the protactile movement continues to spread and transform.

4.8 Conclusion

In this chapter, I have analyzed interviews, ethnographic field notes, and archival materials in order to provide an account of the inception of the protactile movement in Seattle, Washington, in the 2010s. This movement has since grown in many ways that could not have been predicted at the time I conducted this research, and in places I am unfamiliar with. This chapter is not meant to be a comprehensive or complete account. Precisely the opposite: It is meant to highlight the historically and culturally specific dynamics that gave rise to protactile principles and practices in Seattle. It is an open question how historical and cultural dynamics elsewhere will affect the protactile movement wherever it touches down and takes root. Further research will surely uncover new understandings of what it means to be protactile and what conditions must be in place to enable that process.

In the next chapter, I focus on the role of language in reinforcing new, protactile ways of being. This shifts attention from *residing in* to *representing* the world. At the center of analysis is an emerging "deictic" system, or linguistic system used to direct attention to objects in the immediate environment. In analyzing conditions that give rise to that system, I focus on a moment when patterns in how people reside in the world exert pressure on the internal structure of language. While the newness of the language in this case is highly unusual, it foregrounds something that is surely true for us all: At any given moment in history, there will be some restricted set of options for how we can be, and every time we refer to, or talk about, anything at all, we must choose just one of those options. Given this, reference can operate like a switch, which, due to its seeming simplicity and concreteness, can push people toward one way of being or another, without any explicit mention of identity, language, or other common topics of political discourse.

5
Being for Speaking

In the previous chapter, I described how the protactile movement emerged in the Seattle DeafBlind community and how it exerted pressure on the organization of interaction and language-use. I traced the emergence of new communication conventions in particular social and institutional contexts, and I showed how, through pedagogy and politics, a new and more tactile world began to take shape. Implicit in this story are some important questions about the way a person uses language, on the one hand, and the way the world appears to the speaker of that language, on the other. While there are many different ways of thinking about the complex interaction of language and the world, in this chapter, my point of departure is the idea that our thoughts are prospectively oriented toward acts of speaking—a process known as "thinking for speaking" (Slobin 1996). Scholars who have analyzed thinking for speaking across languages have noted that each language has a grammar and each grammar has requirements for which aspects of experience must be expressed. Therefore, "[w]hatever else language may do in human thought and action, it surely directs us to attend—while speaking—to the dimensions of experience that are enshrined in grammatical categories" (Slobin 1996: 71).

In this chapter, I extend this line of inquiry to argue that pressures exerted during the process of language-use lead protactile DeafBlind people not only to attend to their environment in particular ways, but to *be* in their environment in particular ways. This is most evident when they are engaged in a special kind of language-use called, "deictic reference." As I explained in Chapter 1, deictic reference is a kind of "pointing," carried out using terms like *I* and *you*, *here* and *there*, *this* and *that*, which are unusual when compared to other kinds of words, because in order to interpret them, two values must be retrieved—one from the linguistic system and the other from the immediate environment. If someone says, "house," you have some sense of what they mean, whether or not there is a house before you. In contrast, if someone says "I," requirements for interpretation are more complex. First, you must know that "I" means "the person currently speaking." Second, you must be able to locate the person in the speech situation who is speaking at the time the word "I" is uttered. For example, if I were to ask a DeafBlind person, "Should we sit *there* or *there*?," I must (a) know the linguistic form conventionally associated with the concept *there* as well as any alternate concepts I could have chosen, but didn't (e.g. *here*); (b) be able to *be* here in much the same way you are; and (c) identify a pathway or relation from *here* to *there* for *us*. While something like this is required for anyone speaking deictically (Hanks 2009), the present ethnographic context highlights the fact that we must commit to being one way or another before we can refer to, or talk about, anything at all. In other words, historically and culturally given possibilities for how we can be are prospectively oriented to acts of speaking—hence: *being for speaking*.

In order to arrive at a more thorough understanding of being for speaking and its consequences, I begin by reviewing some of the ideas central to *thinking* for speaking (Section 5.1). In Sections 5.2 and 5.3, I review the institutional histories that generated options for how DeafBlind people in Seattle could be before and after the protactile movement. These sections focus on a historical moment when DeafBlind people were faced with a choice between old ways of being DeafBlind and new ways of being DeafBlind. In Section 5.4, I argue that because grammatical structure encodes social choices like this, and because it has a special capacity to repetitively impose those choices on its speakers, language can act as a catalyst, pushing people toward one way of being or another.

5.1 Thinking for Speaking

Does the language you speak influence your perceptions of reality? This is a question that has occupied the minds of cultural anthropologists since the inception of the field. Franz Boas, a foundational thinker in this tradition, encountered this question as he described the difficulty hearing people have in perceiving sounds when they occur in a novel or unfamiliar context. He called this "sound-blindness" and argued that it is a pervasive condition of spoken-language communication (Boas 1889: 47–49). Sound-blindness is the negative product of many years of learning how to produce and hear the sounds in a particular language. When a speaker produces those sounds, the actual positions of the speech organs are not the same each time, due to various idiosyncratic circumstances (a dry mouth, a loud environment, allergies), and this means that individual sounds are not the same across instances of use. How, then, does the hearer recognize sounds produced by different people in different contexts?

Boas says that the hearer can only recognize a sound because she has heard a similar sound before and judges it to be more similar to that sound than to some other sound she has previously heard. In Boas's words, if a sound is understood as similar to one that has been heard before, "the difference between the two stimuli will be so small that it does not exceed the differential threshold" (Boas 1889: 48–49). And he clarifies further: "It will be understood that I do not mean to say that such sensations are not recognized in their individuality, but they are classified according to their similarity, and the classification is made according to known sensations" (ibid.: 50). For example, in learning a new language it is likely that mistakes will be made due to a misapplication of the categories of the native language. Anyone who has attempted to learn a second language will be familiar with the problem: Your language teacher pronounces a word in the language you are learning and asks you to repeat it. You repeat what you think is the same word, but your teacher shakes his head and asks you to try again. He is hearing something that you are not hearing.

William Stokoe (1960) and several generations of linguists since him have demonstrated that the same is true of visual languages. For example, in ASL, the signer can produce the verb "to see" in a range of locations on the face. However, if the location slips below some threshold, it becomes the verb "to smoke." Distinguishing between the two is, in part, a matter of determining whether, on a given occasion, the sign in question is closer to what the signer has previously interpreted as "see" or "smoke." In moments like these, it becomes clear that we do not hear or see the sounds or gestures of language as straightforward, physical stimuli. Instead, we compare them to sounds and gestures we have encountered before, and as Boas argued, we recognize them as falling within a minimum threshold of sameness or difference. Language, then, involves categories and relations that are imposed on the physical phenomena of vocal and manual gesture. If we think of these "raw materials" as being part of a language-external reality, the particular language we speak renders certain dimensions of that reality perceptible and others imperceptible. In other words, the language we speak influences our perception of reality.

Edward Sapir, a student of Boas, extended this idea further. He argued that each form in a language has a corresponding "feeling," which derives from its relation to other forms in the same language (Sapir 1995 [1934]: 155). For example, in ASL there is a sign that is often glossed "worse." At first glance, this word has the same meaning as the English word "worse." However, the following use of the term "worse" is possible in ASL and not in English: "Joe is a pretty good photographer, but Julie is worse good." This is because the meaning of the ASL word "worse" overlaps with the meaning of the corresponding English term. However, unlike the English term, it derives its value, in part, from its formal similarity to the ASL word "multiply." In its association with "multiply," the ASL word "worse" can be positive or negative (it just means more), while the English term is always negative. Sapir would say that the meaning of the ASL and English terms are overlapping, but their "form-feeling" is different. This difference does not derive from states of affairs in the world but from the relation of one sign to another within the same language.

According to Sapir, words are always caught up in relations like this, so even though two words in two different languages might refer to the same object, their form-feeling will always differ. These differences build up, so that users of a language orient to objects in the world through distinct sets of "form-feeling coordinates." These coordinates, through habitual use, lead to a certain "feeling for relations." This relational intuition begins in speaking a language, but it extends further, with use, to constrain conceptualization and organize sense-perception. For Sapir, then, the study of language is, to some degree, the study of the way the world appears to the language-user.

Building on the work of Boas, Sapir, and others working in the same tradition, psychologist and linguist Dan Slobin (1996), proposed a shift from the static concepts of "thought" and "language" to the dynamic concepts of "thinking" and "speaking." Instead of an atemporal snap-shot view of the linguistic system and the reality outside of it, Slobin focuses on the moment of speaking, as it unfolds in time. He argues that in formulating our utterances in that moment, we engage in a kind of thought that is prospectively oriented to the grammatical resources available in the specific language we are speaking. Thought can take many forms, but, Slobin writes, "we encounter the contents of the mind in a special way when they are being accessed for use" (76). In other words, the kind of thinking that takes place in the activity of language-use involves selecting aspects of experience that can readily be conceptualized and coded in the language we are speaking.

Scholars of language and gesture have since pointed out, however, that language is not the only resource available for the expression of thought (McNeill and Duncan 2000). They have demonstrated that the gestures hearing people produce while they are speaking, or "co-speech gesture," are systematically synchronized with speech such that language and gesture must be considered "co-expressive" (p. 2). This tightly integrated paring of language and gesture enables speakers to conceptualize and formulate their thoughts in terms of both the "categorical" requirements of language, and the "imagistic" possibilities of gesture. For example, in describing an event, one must decide if the event has been completed or is ongoing if the language being spoken at that moment has a verbal affix for each meaning and one or the other must be chosen. This kind of choice is characteristic of language as a semiotic system. According to McNeil and Duncan (2010), gesture is different from language in that it does not present the speaker with such choices. Instead, it offers a kind of synthetic glue, which helps unite linguistic elements in a larger semiotic expression, which, as a whole, shares important characteristics with the represented objects (pp. 3–4). In this view, speech and gesture are not redundant nor is one a "translation" of the other. Rather, the minimal processing unit for the expression of thought is a synthesis of the two: it is "imagistic-categorial" in nature (p. 7).

In this chapter, I argue that speaking deictically, more than any other kind of speaking, works to integrate residence and representation because it links language to the world, as it is habitually grasped by its speakers. Consider a deictic expression like "this one" in English. In producing this expression, the speaker's intentional status is filtered through the expressive possibilities of the deictic system of English. The meaning of the word *this* derives from the convention that in English, *this* is not *that*. Because the contrast between the two is highly schematic, a gesture, such as pointing, would also be required to pick out one among many possible referents. However, producing "this one" (and the gesture that goes with it) in a way that is interpretable requires more than language and gesture, for at least two reasons: First, in order to individuate an object of reference in the immediate environment, it has to be there. Second, we must be here in much the same way to presuppose a pathway or relation from here to there for *us*.

5.2 Ways of Being DeafBlind

Recall that when I say "way of being," I am drawing on Paul Kockelman's theory of the "residential whole." Building on the philosophy of Martin Heidegger, Kockleman argues that residing in the world involves a chain of activity that starts with interpreting the environment in terms of "affordances." "Instruments" with particular affordances are wielded to perform actions. If certain actions are performed routinely, a role is taken on, and taking on certain roles habitually leads to a way of being. There are conventional associations involved at each step in that process, so it is not as if you can be whoever you like. The options for how we can be are historically and culturally given, and yet we are also active interpreters of our own being. According to Heidegger, that is what sets us apart as human—that our being is, as he says, an "issue" for us. He doesn't mean that we have an explicit awareness of our being. He emphasizes that our being is an issue for us, in a vague and everyday way. It is something we acquire unwittingly as part of socialization and it operates at the threshold of conscious awareness, so to us and to others, it feels like: *That's just who I am.*

Although it wasn't Heidegger's focus, one's way of being continues to develop through the life course and can do so in rapidly changing conditions, such that a break in transmission or development occurs, and a new way of being is needed and made possible. As I have mentioned in previous chapters, most of the DeafBlind people in this book were born Deaf and slowly became blind over the course of several decades. They were socialized in Deaf communities and learned a visual language, but usually around adolescence they began the slow process of becoming blind. They ended up in adulthood in a world that their socialization had not prepared them for, having to find some way to be.

I am not claiming that situations like this are unusual. Adolescents elsewhere transition to adulthood under conditions of rapid historical change, where their options for how to be are in flux and there is a sense of newness to their trajectory. Sometimes political or economic systems collapse, for example, and with them the structures of authority that ground practice. In that case, people of all ages have to find new ways of being what they used to be, what they planned to be, or else forge some other path by interpreting their environment in new ways—seeing new affordances in the things around them. At that point, possibilities for action shift, a reconfiguration of social roles is triggered, and new ways of being can emerge.

Over the years conducting research in DeafBlind communities, I have watched many people arrive at a crossroads, where it is clear to them and to those around them that they need to find a new way of being; but from the 1970s to now the options available to them once they have that realization have shifted dramatically. When people in the 1970s were told they would go blind, they couldn't imagine how life could go on at all. No one explained to them what they could expect or how they might cope. When methods of coping with blindness were recommended, they were often unappealing. For example, two DeafBlind sisters reportedly sought advice from a prominent Deaf teacher in the 1970s, when they were teens and just starting to become blind. He told them that once they were blind, they would have to sign in a smaller and smaller space to accommodate their shrinking tunnel of vision, and at the end they would have to switch to fingerspelling. He said that sign language would no longer be a possibility once they were blind.

Given projections like this, it was difficult to imagine how life would be possible at all.

Growing up as a Deaf child with "vision problems" meant being picked on by other kids, being called clumsy, and being treated as not smart or not capable because of misunderstandings surrounding vision. Blindness was what made you not a good athlete, not a graceful person, not smart, but it was not clear, in a positive sense, what life might be like as a "blind Deaf person." Against this background, Seattle appeared as a place with hope for a collective future and energy for building it. Blindness was not stigmatized the same way that it was in the broader Deaf community. There were recognizable social roles to be inhabited and people to hang out with. Seattle became a rare and viable alternative to many of the effects of blindness, though not exactly as a place where blindness could be embraced. Counter-intuitively, cultivating a "DeafBlind" identity led not to a shared world suited to tactile experience but rather to services and social roles that would keep impending blindness at bay (Chapter 3).

5.3 New Ways of Being "Tactile"

In the 20 years after the DeafBlind Service Center (DBSC) was established (Chapter 2), a few key events transpired that led to new tactile ways of being. While an in-depth analysis is provided in Chapter 4, key points are as follows: First, the national standards for certifying sign language interpreters changed in 2005. Instead of requiring a two-year associate's degree, they were now requiring a bachelor's degree. As a result, the interpreter training program at Seattle Central Community College closed and nothing replaced it. Almost immediately the shortage of interpreters was felt, and the situation worsened quickly. Second, Adrijana was hired as the first ever DeafBlind director of DBSC in that same year, 2005. Recall that at that point in the history of the community, DeafBlind people could be "tactile," which meant they communicated by touching the hands of the person who was signing, or they could be "tunnel-vision," which meant they communicated visually, through a restricted channel. Up until this point, it was the tunnel-vision people who were offered the best jobs, were the first to know of any news or gossip, and were invited to all of the best parties and events. Tunnel-vision people were closer to the center of things, and the center of things was sighted. The better one was at approximating sighted norms, the more access one had. However, Adrijana was a tactile person, and she responded to the shortage of interpreters from a tactile perspective.

Lastly, Adrijana hired more tactile DeafBlind people than any previous director had, so there were groups of tactile people routinely working together. At the time, tactile people communicated with each other through interpreters, so when they needed to have a meeting among themselves, they had two options. They could wait for several weeks for an interpreter to be available (and wait times were always getting longer), or they could have their meetings without interpreters and try to communicate as a group, directly. Adrijana and her staff chose the latter option, which meant they had to find new ways to communicate. They figured things out as they went and they didn't realize how much their communication practices had changed until people from the Lighthouse visited and the DBSC staff found that "they didn't know how to communicate." After a period of confusion, Adrijana and her team concluded that the DBSC staff had "gone tactile" while the Lighthouse workers had not, and this was the root of the problem. Once they identified that difference, they created a politics around it. They called what they were doing "protactile" and what the Lighthouse was doing "not protactile." This distinction went far beyond communication. They argued, in the broadest terms, that to be protactile is to act on the assumption that hearing and vision are totally unnecessary for life. All human activity can be realized via touch.

They made these assertions, but they didn't actually know how protactile walking, cooking, eating, or communicating would work. So as a kind of experiment Adrijana and DBSC's education specialist, Lee, started organizing DeafBlind-only events. They argued that DeafBlind people have stronger intuitions about touch than sighted people do, but their intuitions had been buried by sighted socialization. The first step, then, was to get rid of the interpreters and try to do things together. They organized classes where one DeafBlind person would teach others how to use a saw, or how to make a milkshake, and without interpreters, communication had to be direct. At first, the idea of getting rid of sighted mediators was unpopular, but Adrijana and Lee pushed. When people announced that they were going back to the old system because they had been touched in a way they felt was inappropriate, they were told: Do you think when a sighted person gets a dirty look, they give up on vision altogether? When people said they were overstimulated by all of the touching, they were told that their response was an effect of social isolation and they should fight through it. One by one, they converted the members of their community like that, and then their interpreters, their families, and their friends. They called their effort the "protactile movement"(Chapter 4).

As the protactile movement gained ground, DeafBlind people encountered new choices. Rather than choosing between being tactile or tunnel vision, now one chose to be protactile or not-protactile. Status accrued to all things protactile, which meant that those who embraced the protactile way of being had greater access to social networks, information, employment, and other valuable resources. Awareness of this shift spread more quickly than the practices themselves, so people started claiming they were protactile, but this only got you so far. At some point, adopting the label would not be enough. You would have to know how to *be* protactile. One place where this tension surfaced was in language-use, and in particular moments when referents in the immediate environment were singled out using special linguistic resources tailored to the task.

5.4 Being for Speaking

By the time the protactile movement started to take root in the mid-2000s, I was already away at graduate school. I returned during summer and winter breaks. On one of those visits, I saw something unusual. An interpreter, walking with a DeafBlind person, was describing something, and as part of her description she was pointing. The DeafBlind person interpreting the description cut her off mid-sentence and told her that the way she was pointing was incorrect. She then modeled a new kind of pointing (the "correct" kind) which involved incorporating the other person's body into the expression (as I describe below). Several things about this encounter were unusual. First, the force and confidence with which the DeafBlind person intervened and the decisiveness with which they evaluated one practice over another as correct; second, the way the interpreter accepted the intervention without question; and not least of all this new way of pointing, which was unlike anything I had ever seen. In retrospect, I recognize this as an early sign that DeafBlind people were taking up residence in the world in new and more tactile ways, and new affordances in their environment were being discovered. From there, they started replacing sighted people as the experts on tactile communication, and as a result communication started to make a lot more sense.

Prior to the protactile movement, sighted people were the experts. It was common for DeafBlind people to pretend that they understood sighted people's descriptions—maybe to avoid derailing the interaction, or maybe to avoid becoming a "difficult DeafBlind person" whom interpreters didn't want to work with. As DeafBlind leaders started training members of their community, they emphasized the importance of DeafBlind people being the ones to decide what was and wasn't clear. To do that, they often turned to activities involving pointing, such as direction-giving, for which comprehension could easily be verified (either you understood my directions to the door and could locate it or you didn't). The strategies that DeafBlind people had relied on for keeping up appearances were thereby challenged and an alternative (one that was actually effective) was proposed.

Before the protactile movement, pointing involved extending a finger toward the referent, along a visual pathway, just as one would expect in ASL. In protactile workshops, this type of pointing was proven ineffective and deemed inappropriate by the instructors, Adrijana and Lee. "Protactile philosophy" became a way of legitimizing new practices as they were emerging. For example, in the following exchange Adrijana demonstrates to her student that he can't resolve reference using ASL pointing signs and she explains that this failure is predictable from the perspective of protactile philosophy:

ADRIJANA: I'm going to explain PT philosophy to you. I'm not going to preach. It's going to be a discussion between the two of us. So let's say that I come up to you, and I start explaining: "There's a table over there, and there's a door further over there." Do you understand me?

DB PARTICIPANT: Yes.

ADRIJANA: No you don't.

DB PARTICIPANT: You said that there is a wall over there [points] and a door over there [points] right?

ADRIJANA: No, the door is over there [points].

DB PARTICIPANT: Well, whatever.

ADRIJANA: Yeah, but that's exactly it. It's important. When people point like that to direct you, and you're standing in the middle of the room, you're totally lost. Right? [DB participant nods]. You're sitting here, and it might seem clear for a minute, but when you stand up and try to find the things I just located for you, the directions won't seem to match the environment and you'll be confused. Deaf [sighted] people do that—they point to places, but that's not clear.

DB PARTICIPANT: Well, yeah. That's visual information.

ADRIJANA: Right. But it has to be adapted to be protactile. So instead of pointing, we have to teach them to do this. . . .

To direct her DeafBlind interlocutor to the door, Adrijana produced an expression foreign to ASL. Instead of extending a finger out into space along a visual trajectory, Adrijana took the DB participant's hand and turned it over so the palm was facing up. She held it in place with her left hand from underneath. Then, with her right hand, she located herself and her interlocutor by pressing a finger into the upturned palm to mean "here." Then, she touched her finger first to her interlocutor's chest (meaning "you") and touched her own chest to mean, "me." This sequence can be glossed, "here, you, me," and the translation would be, "You and I are here."

This is a representation of the ground, against which, something in the environment is singled out. Once Adrijana established this as "our" location (i.e. her and her student), by pressing on her student's palm, she could then locate the door relative to that location. First, she presses the thumb of her left hand into the location she has associated with "here," and keeps it pressed down. Then, she traces a path from "here" to the door. Finally, she presses once in the location associated with the door, to mean "the door is here in relation to us." As the deictic system of protactile language emerged, a systematic contrast across speakers emerged between "press" and "trace," where the former represents a discrete location in space, and the latter represents a path (Edwards 2015). This is a "locative" set, or a set of terms that provides different ways of describing locations. In this two-term set, contrast is based on the presence or absence of a path. This is a highly salient dimension of proprioceptive experience across contexts since one knows, without any visual or sonic input, if they are experiencing movement along some path or not. For that reason, this contrast is a good candidate for incorporation into the deictic system of the language.

This schematic set of linguistic meanings, and others like it, are made specific when a term in the set is instantiated, or used, just as "I" (the person speaking) is made specific when it is associated with the person speaking in the speech situation. The facts of the situation, as they appear in the interaction, accrue to schematic distinctions and are anticipated by language, but they are not *in* language. In the example given above, the linguistic system provides a simple and relatively abstract contrast: ± path movement. + path movement = "trace," − path movement = "press." This contrast is then applied in a specific interaction between two protactile people. The specific path that is traced is not supplied by the language.

For a visual person standing in the middle of a room, the walls, the floor, and the ceiling have affordances for navigation. We can see where the door is relative to us because there is a floor, a ceiling, and walls—all of which give us a sense of orientation. From here to the door is a straight line that follows our sightlines. For a DeafBlind person who has gone tactile, the first move would be to find some orienting, tactile structure instead. If there is only one texture, such as carpet, on the floor, the floor itself is not helpful. It would therefore be necessary to seek out a place where two textures or structures come together, such as the wall and the floor. The place where the wall meets the floor constitutes an orienting line, sometimes called a "shoreline." Protactile deictics anticipate these patterns in how affordances are interpreted for purposes of navigation and project tactile motor lines, not sightlines.

This system emerged when protactile people started communicating directly with each other and interpreters were not around to sort out misunderstandings. In the following exchange, for example, Adrijana is with another student. They are on a break from the workshop, and the student mentions that one of the sighted videographers, Victor, is nearby. He points in the direction of where he thinks Victor is using ASL. Adrijana responds by saying, "You see Victor? I don't see anything." Then the student tries, unsuccessfully, to clarify. Adrijana appears irritated. She puts down the bottle of water she has been drinking and prepares to intervene in a way that became familiar to me, analyzing videos from protactile workshops. I began to think of these moments as more than mere corrections. They seemed to be treated as a test to determine if the person would choose an old way of being DeafBlind or if they would be open instead to a new, protactile way of being. In this case, Adrijana explains that he needs to locate Victor in the protactile way and she demonstrates. She takes his dominant hand and turns it palm-up. Then she presses her finger into her student's chest and then her own chest to mean "you and me." The student can feel her pointing to her own chest because he has a "listening hand" attached to her articulating hand. Then she presses on the palm of his other hand to mean "here." Finally she says "Victor" and presses on several places on the palm, followed by a question marker to mean: "Which of these locations is it? Where is Victor in relation to us?"

In order to interpret deictic expressions like these and respond in a way the teacher will accept, the student has to be protactile. He has to inhabit the environment he is in a more tactile way and that shift is thrust upon him. It isn't a matter of personal preference or a step in his personal process of becoming blind. The language requires him to be protactile in that moment. When people are becoming blind slowly, they adapt slowly, bit by bit. However, every time a referential situation like this unfolds, a kind of pressure is exerted that takes a slow gradual process and turns it into a *switch*. You are either prompted to cash in on the visual affordances in your environment or you are prompted to cash in on tactile affordances, and each of those choices comes with a cascade of consequences for who you are and who you are taken to be. At some level, people choose. But if someone gives you directions to the door in protactile language, you have to commit, in that moment, to being protactile just to interpret the instructions. This is what I am calling "being for speaking," where one's way of being in the world is structured by categories and relations encoded in the language being spoken.

I am not claiming that new ways of being DeafBlind emerge moment to moment in the unfolding of specific interactions. As I have argued, the options DeafBlind people have at their disposal, in any one speech situation, are socio-historical products. In the 1980s, prior to the protactile movement, the options were very different than they are now, and those differences have been shaped in part by the convergence of institutional histories at the Seattle Lighthouse for the Blind and Seattle Central Community College. These institutions together generated conditions that made it possible for DeafBlind people to avoid contact with each other. Without that, it would have been difficult for visual ways of being to persist as long as they did. New ways of being emerged when there were no longer enough interpreters to maintain that system, and, crucially, when actors in key positions of authority were tactile DeafBlind people. In situations where DeafBlind leaders want to convert people to new ways of being DeafBlind, deictic reference plays a key role.

While acts of deictic reference make these requirements impossible to ignore, Adrijana and Lee drew their students' attention to this consistently across all sorts of contexts, even those where language-use was not the primary activity. For example, in a lull between activities in the protactile workshops, Lee was trying to teach a small group of students, but she kept getting interrupted by people asking her questions. After the third interruption, there was some confusion among her students. They couldn't understand what was going on. One person in the group responded to the confusion by reverting to vision. He leaned back and started looking around with his eyes, while the rest of his body was still (and therefore, from a tactile perspective, disengaged). Lee tapped him to get his attention and said:

> Don't just stand there, passively, and look around. You have to be actively seeking information through touch. If someone isn't interpreting information, and you're just standing there, knowing you are missing out on information, you have to do something about it. Does PT mean that everyone has to wear a blindfold and never use their eyes for anything? Not at all! The point is to always communicate through touch. If you're just standing back getting information visually, it means you don't respect PT.

For Lee, "respecting PT" meant getting information in ways that generate information for others. This yields, in Goffman's terms, a "situation," which he defined as "a space of mutual monitoring possibilities" (1964: 135). To "be here" means, minimally, monitoring the situation in ways that could be monitored by others, and more specifically, in ways that presuppose tactile modes of access. If a person is just standing there, perfectly still (apart from an undetectable back and forth of the eyes), they are essentially exiting the situation. The point, Lee explains, is not to deny one's biological capacity to see (if one has remaining sight). It is to actively enter into a space of mutual monitoring possibilities by choosing channels that can be presupposed across the group. A few moments after this interaction, perhaps feeling bad for the pointed correction, Lee shifts to a more understanding tone and says, "I know, I completely get it. We are telling you a lot about what protactile is, and you are getting it, intellectually, but it takes a while for it to go from something you are thinking about to something you are." This intervention suggests that once the channels that can be presupposed across the group are internalized, reaching one's hands out to gather tactile information in a moment of interactional confusion will become as natural as glancing across the room in response to a visual disturbance.

The level at which Lee and Adrijana intervened left space for their students to uncover new affordances in the environment that had previously gone undiscovered. They were insisting that everyone "be here," not that they adopt this or that specific practice or "technique." Almost immediately, though, Lee and Adrijana's interventions were mistaken for more rigid attachments. For example, at one point, Lee was teaching two new students that they should give the speaker tactile feedback (such as tapping on or squeezing their thigh). In one-on-one conversations, the students were picking it up, but when there were three people, they faltered. In one such case, Lee reminded her students to give tactile feedback. They asked her exactly what they were supposed to do with their hands. They asked, "What is the 'right way' to do it?" Lee responded, "It doesn't matter. I'm not trying to give you specific rules to follow. It's just the principle— it's important for the person talking to feel the feedback. Exactly how you do that is up to you." The emphasis is not on doing things in a particular way because you are in a protactile environment, i.e. being appropriate to context, but on creating a context that would make all kinds of actions legible and effective. At the most basic level, this involved simply *being there*.

One of the most fundamental structures that effectively yielded a sense of being there was a particular configuration for two-person interactions. Prior to the protactile movement, utterances were conveyed from the hands of the speaker to the hands of the addressee, and these were usually the only parts of their bodies in contact. Just weeks into the workshops, a new contact surface became conventional, which greatly expanded the number and types of available channels. Instead of the hands being the only point of contact, speaker and addressee sat with their faces just a few inches from one another, legs touching on one side, on the outer thighs. This increase in proximity and surface area meant that behaviors could be observed, recognized, and typified via thermal, motoric, olfactory, proprioceptive, and touch-based channels. It turns out that some people heat up when they are exerting effort or are experiencing emotional strain, while others do not. You can tell what kind of soap they use to wash their clothes, whether they have a dog, and what kind of foods they cook at home. If one were to exit the situation (to silently move the eyes around in their sockets, for example), those channels, and all of the information they carry, would retract or grow thin, and the existence of the other would be attenuated.

Recall that the word "I" cannot be interpreted until the person speaking has been located in the immediate environment. This raises an important question: Is there a minimal threshold of existence for being a speaker? Can the speaking "I" be merely a set of disembodied hands, floating around in air space? Even if your answer to this question is yes, consider the fact that a speaker is only a speaker in relation to an addressee. If the legs are continuously pressed together from the beginning to the end of the encounter, the thigh of the speaker is readily accessible to the addressee's hand for sending signals that they are listening and engaged. Without any way to register the fact that you are being addressed, can you really be an addressee? If there is no addressee, how can there be a speaker? Perhaps this explains Adrijana and Lee's intuition to start with co-presence. Do whatever it takes to be here together. From there, a wealth of affordances will be revealed for actions of all kinds.

Given this approach, new roles quickly became available. There were new ways of participating in conversation, giving or attending lectures, workshops, and dinner parties. There were new ways of playing and watching games, and if one wanted to observe some other activity, protactile people had intuitions about how that might be done. For example, during the workshops, Adrijana wanted to teach participants how to make macramé sleeves for bottles, mugs, and other household objects (instead of "boring" Braille labels). While she manipulated long strands of twine, her students would stand behind her, their arms and hands placed on top of her arms and hands, so they could track every movement, while also feeling the effects on the twine. In order to make that feasible, the students had to press their chests against their teacher's back, resting their chin on her shoulder. Elsewhere, that kind of contact would only be appropriate in the context of an intimate relationship, but, here, that was the structure that effectively incorporated and contextualized the relevant role-relation, and therefore it was quickly and widely adopted. All of this structure depended on the ability to be a speaker and an addressee.

From within those structures, signs of attention, agreement, boredom, interest, annoyance, and confusion came through loud and clear. This meant that in speaking and being spoken to in the context of a particular activity, one could, for example, be annoying, a good student, a keen observer, or a boring person. The primary roles of speaker and addressee were incorporated into and contextualized by a wide range of participation frameworks (which are discussed below). Within those frameworks, more specific and contingent roles emerged as patterns of behavior were consistently observable and therefore typifiable (Hanks 1990; Irvine 1996). In an interview, Lee explained how this process was set in motion as reliance on sighted people was reduced:

> If an object is in front of a DeafBlind person, an interpreter is very likely going to explain the object to them. [...] The more DeafBlind people are in contact with other DeafBlind people, the more tactile things will become. The more tactile things become, the more DeafBlind people will demand that kind of thing from interpreters. For example, the DeafBlind person touches the object and then asks the interpreter a bunch of questions about it. That's so much better than the other way around. So really there is a reversal of information—where it originates. Sighted people make less decisions about what counts as information, so there is less chance for them to impose their visual perspective.

Again, this goes back to the two basic requirements Lee and Adrijana insisted upon. First, DeafBlind people must know how to be co-present. Second, DeafBlind people decide together what counts as relevant or worthwhile information, which is a process that must be ratified by the members of the group over time. Together, these requirements guarantee that representations of the world will always be grounded in tactile ways of being in the world. Deictic reference is a productive activity for generating, reinforcing, and testing those connections.

5.5 Conclusion

In this chapter, I have argued that the protactile movement introduced new options for how one could be DeafBlind. In the early stages of the movement, when ways of being were in flux, new and emerging linguistic systems in protactile language, and in particular the deictic system, played a crucial role by encoding social choices and then recycling and re-imposing those choices moment to moment, day to day, at the periphery of awareness. There is a subtle relentlessness to this that can push people down a path they might otherwise take later, more slowly, or not at all. Adrijana and Lee developed a reflexive awareness of this and they used it to propagate a social movement. In particular, when they wanted to convert a member of their community to a protactile way of being, they often employed deictic reference. This, more than any other form of language-use, forced their interlocutors to be protactile.

Since then, the deictic system of protactile language has become a repository for regularities in navigation, interaction, and communication and it demanded that values be returned from that order. For example, two different combinations of movement and contact, "tap" and "press," systematically invoke different dimensions of setting (Edwards 2015). "Tap" is a demonstrative. It singles out a referent against a horizon of other, possible referents (like the English word "this"). "Press," in contrast, is a locative. It identifies a location (like the English word "here"), against a horizon of other, possible locations. There are further contrasts within each category. For locatives, "press" prepares the addressee for a discrete location, while "trace" prepares them for a path. For demonstratives, a trilled "tap" prepares the addressee for a cognitively foregrounded object, while "grip" prepares them for a cognitively backgrounded object. Exposed to this system of contrasts routinely, the addressee becomes sensitive to subtle differences in tactile stimuli in the transmission of linguistic signals in much the same way that in learning a tonal language, one becomes attuned to differences in tone. They also hone sensibilities about how the environment itself is likely to be interpreted. For example, "trace," on its own, includes only the highly schematic concepts: *contact (with a surface)* and *movement (along a path)*. Knowing how to apply those relatively abstract meanings in ways that can be operationalized by one's addressee requires corresponding ways of routinely interacting with environmental structures, such as surfaces and paths that can be used for standing and walking.

In the next chapter, I follow the protactile movement to Gallaudet University in Washington, D.C., where architecture and infrastructure, in the context of urban development, became the focus. At Gallaudet, connections between the structure of the environment and the structure of language were made explicit as an integral part of protactile politics. The challenge was finding a way to be protactile in spaces that were not, and had never been, "for" DeafBlind people. While Seattle was home to DBSC—an organization run by and for DeafBlind people—most places where the protactile movement gained ground, including Gallaudet, had no such institution. At Gallaudet, this problem was addressed by "laminating" protactile environments onto "Deaf Space."

6
The Laminated Environment

In 2016, I conducted 12 months of anthropological fieldwork with Deaf-Blind students, staff, and community members at Gallaudet University in Washington, D.C., in order to understand how protactile principles were interpreted and applied given very different social and historical conditions. In Seattle, as the protactile movement was just beginning, the goal was to suspend sighted judgments about what was appropriate to make room for new practices and norms to emerge. This often meant finding ways for DeafBlind people to be together, away from sighted interpreters, friends, and family (Chapter 4). Despite the general success of those efforts, sighted standards of appropriateness had a way of resurfacing, throwing up obstacles at every turn: chairs that restrict the movements of the arms, tables too big to reach across or move, plexiglass separating customers and cashiers. At Gallaudet, the same sorts of problems were encountered; however, the response was different. In particular, things that would have been treated like annoying obstacles in Seattle were often treated like the outcome of someone's bad decision. I would soon learn that this difference was directly related to "Deaf Space" design, which in 2016 was at the center of public discourse on campus.

Deaf Space, which started in 2005, is an architectural and infrastructural framework for designing buildings, walkways, furniture, systems for modulating light flow, educational technologies, and other structures that support culturally specific navigation and communication practices among Deaf people (Malzkuhn 2007; Bahan 2009; Sangaglang 2012; Hales 2013; Hansel Bauman 2014; Sirvage 2015, 2017; Behm 2019; cf. Kusters 2015). Just a few years after Deaf Space started gaining traction at Gallaudet, the protactile movement touched down (McMillen 2015). Many of the DeafBlind people I knew at Gallaudet were in direct contact with protactile leaders from Seattle and were quickly picking up protactile theory and practice. Deaf Space scholars saw potential in the protactile movement, and they invited people who were involved to work with architects, designers, and administrators to find ways of incorporating protactile perspectives into Deaf Space as the future of the university was re-imagined. The projects they were invited to weigh in on were part of large-scale urban development, which was transforming the area surrounding the university, now known as "NoMa," or "North of Massachusetts Avenue" (MacCleery and Tar 2012). In the next section, I provide background on those projects, which is required to understand the dynamics that were in place when Deaf Space design and the protactile movement converged. While the Seattle DeafBlind community was able to successfully create an independent institution where the protactile movement could grow, most communities will be faced with the problem of taking up residence in someone else's space (Kusters 2015). This chapter analyzes one such case, where "the laminated environment" became a model for co-existence.

6.1 Deaf Space

6.1.1 Urban Development

Urban development projects in the area surrounding the university were funded by a combination of federal and private funds. At the time, the District of Columbia was in federal financial receivership, and "the area represented a vastly underutilized land use asset that was spinning off tax revenues of only about $5 million per year." Therefore, "for the federal government, it was a prime potential site for close-in federal office buildings" and increased tax revenue (MacCleery and Tar 2012). Federal interests dovetailed with those of large private real estate investment companies like JBG Smith, who, according to their 2016 website, specialize in "transit-oriented development" and "submarket dynamics." In the northeast quadrant of Washington, D.C., Gallaudet and the Deaf community surrounding it were one such "submarket." Meanwhile, the president of Gallaudet was working to ensure that the university would benefit from development, rather than fall victim to it.

At the time, Gallaudet was surrounded by a tall, brick wall, and the entryways were guarded by thick, iron gates. There was a security booth at the main gate where vehicles entering the campus had to stop to gain authorized entry. The overall dynamic between the campus and the surrounding community was one of stark separation. Henry, the Director of Campus Design and Planning at the time, explained that as local government invested, and developers started moving in, Gallaudet wanted to ensure that they would benefit from the inevitable "explosion in commerce just outside of the gates." However, breaking down long-standing (physical) barriers also seemed like it would create vulnerabilities. According to Henry, the president of the university started describing the campus as a "99-acre gift" given to the global Deaf community. Framed this way, he said, the stakes were clear, and people understood why the administration "didn't want to sell [the campus] for parts (in fact, one might argue, it wasn't theirs to sell)." This centered the discussion on protection and preservation rather than turning a quick profit. One especially vivid warning that was circulating involved an image: Droves of hearing people flood into campus from the quickly growing residential developments across the street. Once inside, their dogs poop and then they leave.

With unfavorable possibilities like this in mind, the idea of "zones" emerged and gained traction with administrators. Just outside of campus, Deaf and hearing people mix. One rung in, there would be a "buffer zone" where outsiders are welcome, but also have a clear sense that they are visiting a place that is not their own. As they go further into the center of campus, the environment becomes increasingly unwelcoming and impenetrable. Though the precise mechanisms (to my knowledge) had not been worked out, this vision fit with developer's goals of turning NoMa into a "center of culture, creativity, and commerce."

The liminal outer zone was already becoming a reality in 2016 in places like Union Market, a gourmet food hall located across the street from Gallaudet and a few blocks from the NoMa/Gallaudet Metro Station. Deaf and hearing patrons frequented the market, and many of the people who worked there knew enough ASL to get through a routine service encounter. Signed conversations were an integral part of the ambient environment, and hearing patrons had ample opportunity to make themselves understood in new ways. This turned Union Market into a place where people went not just for food, but for a distinctive cultural experience. The presence of Deaf people, their culture, and their practices therefore generated new forms of value for planners and developers (Behm 2019). "Deaf Space" design emerged out of this moment as an intellectual and practical project aimed at creating urban environments with the capacity to reinforce and preserve Deaf culture, while also participating in, and benefiting from, urban development.

6.1.2 Participation

How do people participate in urban development projects? At first it might seem obvious: They attend a focus group or respond to a survey. Deaf Space researchers asked people to do neither. They were interested in the habitual ways that Deaf people move through their environment as they carry out their everyday tasks. So instead of asking people what they did, or what their preferences were, they systematically analyzed video recordings of people walking around, talking, eating, and so forth, and combined those analyses with ethnographic inquiry to draw out patterns in behavior that the people they were studying were aware of peripherally, if at all. Many of these analyses targeted what linguistic anthropologists call "participation frameworks."

Participation frameworks are configurations of roles that people take on in interacting with one another. They can be more or less abstract. For example, the roles of "speaker" and "addressee" are found everywhere language is used and are therefore relatively abstract. In contrast, more specific roles like artist and patron, or student and professor, are tied to particular situations and institutional contexts. The role of "speaker" is always embedded in some more specific role. We do not just speak, we speak in some capacity. However, those connections do not always snap immediately into place in the unfolding of an interaction. For example, if a person approaches me on the street and starts speaking, I know right away that they are a "speaker," but a question may arise soon after: Who are they speaking *as* and what does that make me in this situation?

The problem of how roles like "speaker" and "addressee" come to be embedded in more specific roles like "tourist" and "local," or "teacher" and "student" has been a significant source of debate among scholars of language. Erving Goffman (1981) famously started from the position that the roles of speaker and addressee can be decomposed into constituent roles like the person who authors an utterance, or the "author," vs. a person who relays an utterance someone else has authored, or the "animator." He argued that these roles are then "laminated" in interaction to form a coherent, composite role. Stephen Levinson (1998) later systematized this framework by breaking Goffman's constituent roles down into an elaborate set of interrelated features, increasing the number of roles that could be derived.

Judith Irvine (1996) argued, however, that those who take this kind of "decompositional" approach to role structures have it backwards (pp. 133–134, also see Hanks 1990). Reifying a rigid set of roles or features makes it more difficult to identify roles that fall outside of that set:

> [O]ne might well suspect that the number of such participant roles (PRs) arrived at by the decompositional approach may prove endless. Certainly I can think of some not yet provided for in Levinson's scheme, the most complex decompositional model to date. Consider, for instance, the person quoted against his or her will; the absent party named in an accusation (the "Fingeree"?); the role in a stage play as opposed to the actor playing it; the person a child is named after who may (if living) then have certain specified responsibilities toward the child—all

these possibilities seem to me unrepresented in Levinson's system. We will at least need some way to arrive at further distinctions. Will we end up having to propose "primary" PRs that are highly culture-specific?

Instead of going down that path, Irvine argues that the best approach is to abandon the project of mapping out, in advance, all possible roles, since this often transforms the process that gives rise to roles into a mere "rationale" for the typology. She argues that it is precisely "the process by which participation structures are constructed, imagined, and socially distributed" that should be foregrounded analytically.

If Deaf Space research were boiled down to its most fundamental activity, this might be it: constructing and imagining participation structures, and the complex ways they are laminated onto one another, such that patterns in how Deaf people participate in conversation can become central to how Gallaudet, as an institution, participates in urban development. Unlike linguistic anthropologists, though, Deaf Space designers had to take these analyses one step further, translating them into concrete guidelines for architects and developers. This meant attending not only to participation structures, but also to how those structures interact with affordances in the environment.

After the completion of the first Deaf Space building, the Sorenson Language and Communication Center, or "SLCC," researchers realized they had underestimated the complexity of this task. Sirvage (2017) gives the example of a large, circular bench built into the atrium of the SLCC. He explains that the bench was supposed to be a place where people gathered and conversed, and the atrium where the bench was located was supposed to be the "heart of campus," but after it was built, it was clear that something had gone wrong. The atrium, he explained:

> was too large and empty. People tended to use it as a meeting place. One person would wait there until their friend came down to meet them and then they would leave together. If there were any conversations, they were generally short. They would greet one another, ask how things were going, and then after these brief exchanges, they would go elsewhere to continue their conversation. They never stayed long. Small groups were maybe a little more likely to stay, but even then, people would leave fairly quickly. The only events that lasted were large, formal events that were planned in advance. People would come for the event and then disperse. So the atrium in the SLCC was successful in certain respects, but it didn't become the heart of campus like we had hoped.

It turned out that this problem derived from the fact that early Deaf Space research was based on "external visual observation," and from that perspective, it looked like Deaf people sit and stand in circles when they are in a group conversation. "The bench," explains Sirvage, "was designed around that observation. It traces the contour of a group conversation" (p. 6). However, citing the work of Ben Bahan (2009), Sirvage notes that the:

> contour was calculated using an incorrect geometric formula. From the inside of a Deaf interaction—from the perspective of a person for whom such interactions feel natural—it becomes apparent that... [w]hat we thought was a circle is really flexible overlapping triangles.

When two Deaf people are conversing, they stand opposite one another. When a third person joins, all three participants re-configure their alignment so that two equidistant lines extend out toward each of the other participants. This ensures that all participants are comfortably and reciprocally within the visual field. When additional participants are added, "the underlying organization is still triangular, but more triangles are added, in an overlapping fashion" (Sirvage 2017: 6).

Once this structure had been uncovered, the task for the Deaf Space designer was to understand how to build affordances into the environment to support it. The bench in the atrium of the SLCC was a glaring example of what would happen if they got it wrong. The substitution of rigid surface structure, that could be seen from outside for dynamic underlying structure that could not was a mistake that was literally set in stone. In order to avoid making these mistakes again, Deaf Space design went in a more "imaginative" direction. This led to deeper insights about how Deaf ways of residing in the world were "distinctive," and therefore valuable.

6.1.3 Imagination

In carefully analyzing videorecorded interactions, Deaf Space researcher Robert T. Sirvage didn't just look at surface-level patterns of behavior. He looked at how those behaviors were actually responses to the environment, and the distinct ways it is legible to Deaf people. To communicate his findings, he asks (mostly hearing) Deaf Space architects, planners, and designers to imagine how Deaf people use their eyes to perceive the space behind them.

While hearing people integrate their vision and their hearing for 360 degrees of environmental access, Deaf people, he argues, can only see what is in front of them. He thinks that in order to accommodate that fact, they habitually read shadows on the sidewalk and reflections on glass, are attuned to vibration in the floor, and in crowded environments they will be found with their backs pressed against a wall. Sirvage says that in interaction, each Deaf person "takes responsibility" for the space behind the other person. If they don't, they will be scolded and "[t]hat emotional response tells us that this way of structuring visual attention is not just a biological fact—it has become a cultural rule...". He calls this "Deaf Dorsality" (2015: 4).

Sirvage concluded that a Deaf environment is an environment that minimizes dorsal exposure. Designs based on this insight were then pitched to investors as ways of making the area more architecturally interesting by contributing to a distinctive "Deaf esthetic." For example, Frank, one of the architects I interviewed, described a saw-toothed storefront, where each panel would function like a rearview mirror. Deaf pedestrians walking down the sidewalk could easily glimpse the space behind their head, thereby minimizing dorsality.

Deaf Space depends on significant exposure for hearing architects to Deaf ways of being. This is provided by an expansive network of Deaf scholars, engineers, architects, community members, and university administrators who do the work of exposing. In an interview with one hearing member of the design team, for example, a Deaf supervisor was present and was actively teaching him how to work with interpreters, impressing upon him the importance of learning ASL, and pressing him on his tendency to avoid complex conversations with Deaf members of the design team and favor hearing colleagues instead. This kind of informal educational process, which unfolds in the context of sustained relationships, is essential for a project like Deaf Space. As anthropologist Keith Murphy (2004) has noted, the relations that obtain between the designer and the people they design for are multiply mediated by interactions between members of the design team, such that the object of design emerges, at the outset, in the shared space where co-engagements unfold.

Deaf Space theorists highlight the fact that "empathic" processes are involved, which can play out in face to face interaction, or from a distance. For example, Finnish architect Juhani Palasmaa, who has been influential for Deaf Space practitioners, argues, "Imagination is not a quasi-visual projection; we imagine through our entire embodied existence and through imagination we expand our realm of being" (p. 8). He describes this activity as a kind of intersubjective "tuning" to the eventual inhabitants of the building. Palasmaa's architect doesn't just leave traces of her own activity, she imaginatively experiences the activity of others, and leaves structures for them to find that will support, enhance, or anticipate those activities. Those who occupy the building may or may not be aware of the efforts that led to their experience, and yet, their experience relies on a kind of displaced intersubjective attunement (Duranti 2010; Duranti and La Mattina 2022), which may operate across significant asymmetries (Hanks 2013) and be rooted in an imaginative mode of "sensory access" (Murphy 2015).

6.2 Being Protactile in Deaf Space

In order to understand the recent convergence of Deaf Space and the protactile movement, I interviewed Henry. The interview took place in his office, a large space in a castle-like building that looks out over the rooftops of the campus. He was seated at his desk surrounded by stacks of blueprints, books, and manuals, and behind him was a whiteboard covered in indecipherable markings. Henry told me he had been looking for ways to incorporate feedback from DeafBlind people into Deaf Space projects for years, but it never seemed to work out. Philip, a member of Henry's staff, told me later that he had noticed the same thing.

Phillip explained that a few years earlier, in 2013, he tried to include a group of DeafBlind people in a project involving some curb-cuts on campus. As I mentioned in Chapter 1, curb-cuts are supposed to lead from the sidewalk out into the cross-walk, but because of the way they were angled, they sent people using canes into the middle of the intersection instead. He explained that every time he tried to have a conversation about it with them, confusion set in. "They understood the general problem," he said, "but when we tried to get into the details of how it might be fixed, things deteriorated." One time, he invited a DeafBlind student who was in a leadership role on campus, to talk with him about it. He said:

> I was signing like I always did, and he had his hands on me (he was completely blind). I learned later that that was called "tactile reception of visual ASL". I didn't know that at the time. So I would say something and over and over again, the person would say, "OK, but where is that?" and then they would think for a while. Then they would say, "Where am I now?" I would point this way and then that way and we would walk toward the curb in question, and then the student would say, "Where am I now?" Again, I would point and explain and again they would become confused. I knew he was intelligent and in general a very competent person. I also

knew that he got around on campus on his own, so I couldn't understand what was going so wrong. I realized that the way I framed a discussion about space was flawed from the start. I thought that because he was a good student, got around on his own, he was involved in organizations, he was smart, that he could have an in-depth conversation with me about design. But I didn't realize that there was this huge gap between his experience and the way we were talking about it. Later, when I learned about protactile, it was a huge revelation.

In order for DeafBlind people to exert influence over how the environment was structured, they had to be able to participate in conversations in which various aspects of the environment were referred to. In these moments, a chasm formed between protactile ways of residing in the world and Deaf ways of representing the world. The resources that ASL offered, and more specifically, the categories and relations supplied by its "deictic system," were not up to the task.

6.2.1 "Where Am I Now?"

As I discuss in Chapter 5, a deictic system is a lexico-grammatical system used to direct the attention of others to objects in the immediate environment. In English, deictic expressions include words like *this*, *that*, *here*, and *there*. There is a tradition of analyzing expressions like these in relation to the speaker, who is positioned in time and space. This is an "ego-centric" approach, which is supposed to answer questions like, "Where am I now?" via the conventional oppositions encoded in the deictic system (discussion and review in Hanks 1990). In this view, for example, a speaker might choose *this* when referring to something close, or "proximal" to the speaker, and *that* when referring to something further away, or "distal," with respect to the speaker. Linguists and anthropologists have pointed out, however, that culturally and historically specific patterns in how people interact with their environment, and draw the attention of others to it, can affect the internal organization of the language so that the language comes to anticipate certain aspects of the world as it is experienced by its speakers (Bühler 1934; Evans 2003; Edwards 2014; Cooperider et al. 2016; Sicoli 2016; Diessel and Coventry 2020; Forker 2020). This suggests that the values encoded in a given deictic system cannot be assumed, and there are many more possibilities than just "space" and "time" (Hanks 1990).

In 2016, the protactile deictic system was already emerging, and, as I discuss in Chapter 5, conventional values were encoded that would have been invaluable to Phillip and his interlocutor. Through routine use of the protactile deictic system in a particular setting, the environment takes on certain shared contours. Possible trajectories, locations, and objects cohere to form a world, within which coordinated actions like talking about the design of a curb-cut feel effortless or easy. As Philip's observations suggest, without a functioning deictic system, a shared environment will not be revealed. However, the reverse is also true. Without a shared environment, the deictic system will be inoperable.

In a series of protactile workshops held at Gallaudet in 2016, Adrijana and Lee encountered this problem from the perspective of language acquisition. In a videorecorded instructional session focused on direction-giving, or "mapping," Lee is talking with an undergraduate student who was living on campus. Lee asks for directions to various places nearby and at first it seems that the student can provide them. However, in discussing more detailed options for how to get from place to place, Lee discovers that the student doesn't know basic things about the spatial layout of her surroundings. The student says, "Mapping is a challenge for me because it's hard for me to visualize the things we're talking about." Lee and her student reflected on the fact that the protactile deictic system came with a protactile environment. One reinforced the other.

STUDENT: Mapping is really cool because I didn't know that there are all of these short cuts on campus. I always end up taking the long way—like in the winter, the walk from the dorm to the gym is really cold. I had no idea that you could go through SAC and that there is a door in that building that is really close to the Field House. You don't have to spend all that time in the cold. I wish I had known that before.

INSTRUCTOR: Yeah, so if you had been doing mapping all along it would make everything easier, right? [Student agrees.] We need more people to learn mapping. That's why you're here learning it so you can teach other people. If everyone learned protactile mapping, you could walk up to anyone on campus and ask them for directions and they would be able to tell you in a way that makes sense, rather than pointing to a bunch of different directions in air space. When people start to do that, you can show them how to do it this way.

In subsequent months, DeafBlind people on campus started to acquire protactile language, and in doing so, they were able to point out this, and draw attention to that. Each one of these moments might seem insignificant on its own, but in each referential act, ways of residing in the world and ways of representing the world are aligned, dis-aligned, or otherwise related, yielding a world where DeafBlind people can participate, navigate, negotiate, or just exist.

6.2.2 Affordances in Deaf Space

Some aspects of Deaf Space design already incorporate tactile affordances. One of the first things that came to my attention were "Deaf floors." I learned from Henry, though, that from architectural and engineering perspectives, you can't really talk about "floors" because they are attached to a complex assembly, all of which matters for Deaf Space. One day, he tried to explain it to me. He took out some blueprints, and after rolling them open on his desk he pointed to a place on the drawing and said, "These are trusses.... [T]hey span from here to here and then from here to here, all the way across." Then he pointed out the "underlayment" made of concrete, a "vapor barrier" made of plastic, and the space underneath the building, where there is soil. The soil, he explained, was originally made of clay, which expands when it gets wet, and "that," he said, "can literally destroy a building." To prevent expansion, the top two feet of soil had to be removed and replaced with gravel. On top of all of that trusses there is a 3/4-inch plywood deck, and on top of that there is a material called "gypcrete," which is chalky like drywall, that adds mass to the floor and absorbs most of the sound that is propagated. The goal for Deaf Space is to balance this dampening effect with the transmission of vibrations that can be useful, for example vibrations caused by footfalls. He explained that if the floor let too much information through, it would distract from the information needed to "read" it effectively. "You want control," he said. "So that floor that you're asking me about really includes the whole assembly."

According to Deaf Space guidelines, this assembly is used because it increases the "sensory reach" of the Deaf person standing on the floor by transmitting information that would otherwise be inaccessible, such as a person approaching from behind or a group of people walking past a closed office door. According to Sirvage (2015), Deaf people are attentive to this kind of environmental information and will make use of it wherever it is available. He says:

> If you want to understand what it feels like to be Deaf, you shouldn't wear ear plugs; that would do very little to approximate our experience. What you should do is walk backwards and try to glean cues from your environment to be sure you are walking in a straight line. That way of attending to the environment is a habitual, completely ingrained part of our lives.

In particular, if a group of people is walking down the street, the person most peripheral to the interaction is expected to attend to environmental obstacles. The person speaking is prepared to receive warning signs from that person, as opposed to scanning the environment directly, himself. Designing buildings that anticipate this fact has led Deaf Studies scholars Ben Bahan and Dirksen Bauman to frame architecture as "the third person" in the interaction: "Just as the 'third person' in the group focuses on the path forward and its possible hazards while others focus more intently on the conversation, buildings can *care* for their occupants by providing environmental cues that enhance spatial awareness, safety, and ambient conditions that promote well-being" (italics in the original, cited in Bauman 2014: 388–389).

Protactile people found that Deaf floors also incorporated affordances for them. The dampened vibration they transmitted was something they already attended to, and they pushed designers to use it in other contexts as well, such as built-in benches. I could understand this because on multiple occasions I had enjoyed a particular bench in the hotel on Gallaudet's campus. On top of the bench there are securely attached cushions made of a dense but forgiving material. They carried just enough vibration that you could feel someone sitting on the other end signing, but not so much that it distracted. One day, I was having a conversation on the bench with a member of our group, while two of the others were conversing a few feet down on the same bench. From where I was sitting, I could feel that they were there and that they were having a casual, rhythmic conversation—no urgency, anger, or long lulls were detected. If the bench had been made of concrete, or if the cushions had a different density, that information would have been lost. Deaf Space designers learned from this that materials and assemblies capable of transmitting and dampening vibrations caused by the ordinary activities of others can generate an ambient environment for protactile interaction.

Contrast this with Charlotte's method for creating an ambient environment, discussed in Chapter 1. Nearly a decade earlier in Seattle, I described the details of the coffee shop we were in together using ASL. Just as many others did at the time, I assumed she could use those details to form an impression, based on memories of what coffee shops were like when she was still partially sighted. I was "providing access" to the environment via representations of it. This was necessary in part because of how the environment had been designed, and who the designers imagined would be using it. As I explain in Chapter 1, all avenues to the tactile signs that could have given Charlotte an impression of the place were blocked off. She couldn't get a sense of the coziness of the coffee shop by feeling the condensation on the insides of the windows because there were people sitting at tables, which were positioned under the windows. In order to touch the windows, she would have to lean over the people sitting at the tables, potentially knocking drinks into their laps or otherwise causing a disturbance. She also could have gotten a sense of the atmosphere by touching people's jaws to see if they were eating and if so, how. She could have leaned in to feel the steam coming from their cups. However, the sighted people who designed the coffee shop never imagined that someone like Charlotte would be there.

In 2016 at Gallaudet, the approach was very different. First protactile structures of participation that incorporated relatively abstract roles like speaker, addressee, and non-addressed third party were observed and analyzed. Designers were subsequently advised to incorporate affordances for those patterns in interaction into floors, benches, hallways, and other structures in the environment. For protactile people, this promised to turn Gallaudet into a place that anticipated their existence and invited their participation.

This raises a more general question about what it means to "participate." Recall that linguistic anthropologists have analyzed participation by identifying laminated role-structures and understanding how they relate to the participants who occupy them. Building on more recent approaches to participation that have foregrounded the "environmentally coupled" aspects of communication (Goodwin 2007), protactile design foregrounds the relation between the two and highlights the fact that in order to speak to one another (thereby taking on roles like "speaker") the environment must first speak to us in ways that correspond across the collective. Wherever Deaf Space fulfilled this requirement for DeafBlind people, protactile practices flourished.

One such practice, which had no correlate in Seattle, was "protactile walking." Many of the DeafBlind people I knew at Gallaudet were just beginning the process of becoming blind, and they were looking for activities that would facilitate that transition. They considered "protactile walking" to be one of those activities. Deaf sidewalks are wider than hearing sidewalks in order to support the structure of signed conversations. If you're standing too close, you can't see what the other person is saying. For protactile people, it turned out that those same sidewalks invited groups as large as four people to walk together. After participating in a few of these activities, I discussed them with a DeafBlind member of the group. We recalled the rhythmic coordination of canes and feet, the way it made us feel like a giant spider, and the catalyzing effect those experiences seemed to have on people who were just starting to go tactile.

There were other aspects of Deaf Space that did not support protactile interaction. Some of these conflicts were drawn out at a two-day meeting at

Gallaudet called the "Tactile Mind Research Collaborative." Protactile leaders from across the country were invited to the collaborative to discuss the creative and scientific potential of studying protactile practices with students, staff, and administrators. During those two days, the conversation was not about "access," "inclusion," or "rights." It was about how one environment could be "laminated" onto another such that Deaf and DeafBlind people could co-exist.

6.2.3 The Laminated Environment

The protactile movement seemed to have implications for basic research across nearly every well-represented field at Gallaudet, such as linguistics, cognitive neuroscience, and Deaf studies. "Protactile design" was centered as a way of tying those intellectual strengths to institutional priorities in the context of urban development. John Lee Clark, in an unpublished essay written just after he attended the collaborative, laid out some basic issues that made being on campus not merely unpleasing, but perilous. He said that despite the excitement of the collaborative, "it was depressing to be on campus":

> There were, for example, vast seas of concrete with no tactile landmarks or anything that would provide a sense of orientation and direction. It was also incredibly hard to find any people. I kept asking myself, "Where is everyone?" People seem to have been spread so far apart. It was also a shock to find how difficult it is to get food. [The restaurants and cafes] had glass things in front of the food, and maybe there were workers behind the food, but you couldn't reach them to communicate. There weren't any openings where I could walk around and find one of those workers to find out about food and give my order. The barriers there were absolute and complete, unless I took a chair and climbed over those glass things—I wish I'd thought of doing that when I was there!

The first time I saw a DeafBlind person enter the food service area Clark describes, I was concerned. As a sighted person who had internalized protactile norms, I didn't rush in to help, though (Chapter 1). Instead, I just watched. The DeafBlind person stomped their cane several times on the ground and then waited. After some more waiting and stomping, a sighted Deaf person nearby asked them what they needed and then made sure that they got it. I saw a similar series of events play out in the large, expansive lobby of the SLCC, and again in one of the "vast seas of concrete" in the center of campus.

Being a good Deaf person at Gallaudet, it seemed, was a lot like being a good sighted person before the protactile movement in Seattle (Chapter 4). From a protactile perspective, those sighted interventions drove a wedge between DeafBlind people and their environment. This turned the environment into a description of itself, which, by virtue of passing through the common sense of the sighted mediator, rendered the campus unfamiliar, unknowable, and uninviting. Underlying this model is the insidious notion of "access." Having an informal system that would give you access to restaurants might help you survive (for example locate and consume food), but it would not turn the campus into a place you would want to be.

In trying to find ways for Deaf and DeafBlind people to co-exist, one of the main conflicts that arose during the collaborative and elsewhere was between the "cool visual expansiveness" of Deaf Space and the "compact warmth" of protactile space. In John Lee Clark's words:

> In Deaf Space, open spaces are valued—where people can look around and see things, who's there, talk to someone across the space. Whereas I think the ideal in PT space is that we're happiest when we're like mice running around in a maze, in tunnels. I love walls. How do you put these two together?

Henry discussed this tension as well in an interview. He said that these aspects of protactile environments make it an interesting case, from a design perspective, because, "it might be the one thing that is so incredibly particular that it starts to be exclusive." After pausing to think about that for a moment, he picked up a marker, and turned around toward the white board behind him, and said, "But what's beautiful about that is that one could imagine the built environment is a laminated space. If one of those layers was a DeafBlind layer, you might imagine lines and places" (he drew a rectangle, with little "bubbles" that jutted out from each side). This kind of structure, he said, would form "pathways with eddies," where the pathways would be all about "trailability," and the eddies would be protected spaces that are all about "touch" and "reach."

Addressing this same conflict, Clark added that "where people walk and where their eyes go need not, and probably should not, be the same." Pathways through campus, he said, could easily be given crucial tactile structure by adding a system of railings. Above hip-height, sight lines would be unchanged. For Clark, this would not just be a matter of effective navigation. It would also ensure that two people walking toward each other would converge and have the opportunity to meet, say hi, or ignore each other.

Without common pathways, a Deaf person might realize that a DeafBlind person is present, but the reverse would almost certainly not be true. In subsequent design meetings, people returned again and again to surfaces and the proprioceptive information people pick up through their feet, as ways of laminating one environment onto another. In other words, visual expansiveness and tactile "trailability," when laminated, would yield a shared "situation," or "space of mutual monitoring possibility" (Goffman 1964). This would support the co-existence of Deaf and DeafBlind people.

I learned, as I continued my fieldwork, that this idea of the laminated environment can be extended beyond humans, too. For example, an architect who was working on a Deaf Space dorm at the time explained that toward the end of construction they ran into a problem with the birds. Deaf Space buildings, he explained, generally require more light. This is accomplished by using glass that is more transparent and including more windows. This is great for communication, but "it led to a situation where the birds kept flying into the glass and dying. In other words, it was not a 'bird-safe design'." Unfortunately, you can't correct the problem by adding a reflective layer to the windows because if you do, "the windows reflect the trees; the birds think they are flying into trees and kill themselves that way." In the end, they went with bird houses because the theme for the dorm was "home away from home." For birds, some windows afford death. For Deaf language-users, windows often afford heightened perceptibility in the visual channel. For DeafBlind people, windows might provide a surface that could be traced in navigating from one place to another, which unlike walls might also give off some thermal information about the external environment along the way. Intersecting patterns like these undergird the forms of imagination that architects, urban planners, and designers engage and thematize in Deaf Space, but they also became central to imagining how protactile people could take up residence in a space that was not their own.

6.3 Conclusion

In this chapter, I have extended the notion of "participation," as it has been understood by linguistic anthropologists, to account for environments where Deaf and DeafBlind people were trying to co-exist. The first step in that process was for each group to exist in its own environment, which emerged out of the routine interaction between residence and representation. Only then could designers find ways of "laminating" one environment onto the other to generate new kinds of value for the institution. This approach contrasts starkly with attempts to provide access via representation alone. Questions remain about the sustainability of being protactile in Deaf Space (e.g. McMillen 2015). However, this chapter has captured a brief, imaginative moment in Gallaudet's history, which, in my most optimistic moments, I hope someone might return to and make something of.

7
Conclusions

In reflecting on two decades of anthropological engagement in DeafBlind communities at a time when the protactile movement was taking root, I have arrived again and again at *the limits of language*. Across six interrelated chapters, this book has worked toward a deeper understanding of those limits as a critical site for political intervention, social organization, and ultimately existence itself. I have not set out to establish a conceptual framework that can account for the limits of language once and for all but rather to offer an ethnographic account of what it meant for DeafBlind people in a particular place and time to live their everyday lives without the taken for granted sense that their language and their world would be integrated. One of the many consequences of this was to render fundamental functions of language, such as reference and description, inoperable.

Linguistic anthropology, as a field, grapples with the complex problems that arise at the boundaries of language, as it is analyzed in its complex contexts of use. Where the cut is made between "language" on the one hand and "context" on the other, how each is theorized, and how the relation between the two can be accounted for, is a productive source of debate. For example, some have argued that language is not a coherent object of analysis at all outside of the sequential structure of interaction (Rawls 2002: 11). Others start with a distinction between a "denotational text" (or what has been said in and by discourse) and an interactional text (or what has been done in and by discourse) (Silverstein 2019), where denotation is associated with language and interaction is associated with the effects of language-*use*. This and other contemporary distinctions have been built on earlier theories that distinguish between constructs like *langue* and *parole* (Saussure 1972 [1915]), or competence and performance (Chomsky 1988 [1965]). Each of these distinctions is a first step toward marking a limit beyond which something other than language must become the focus of analysis.

In this book, the primary distinction on which all analysis rests is between *being in the world* and *talking about the world*. Both are understood as semiotic processes, though the constituents involved and the relations between them differ (Kockelman 2006a: 22). The former involves non-propositional content and processes, such as cashing in on affordances in the environment in order to perform actions and in doing so taking on roles, while the latter involves propositional content and processes that are required for description, reference, and depiction (Kockelman 2006a: 22). Taking this distinction as my starting point in analyzing the protactile movement and its effects has led to a re-thinking of several questions of broader anthropological significance.

First, how does the study of meaning or semiotics inform our understandings of social and political action? Propositional statements about the world are a primary means of obtaining resources through established political processes. However, Chapters 2 and 4 foreground the fact that engaging in those processes presupposes and tends to reinforce ways of being in the world that are taken for granted by those in power who govern the political process and establish its parameters. The protactile movement broke from that cycle by turning attention inward to find space away from sighted people, their notions of politeness and appropriateness, and their political frameworks. In that reprieve, the goal was to uncover effective ways of being in the world together and let propositional claims about the world, reality, what is true, what is right and wrong, and what is needed emerge from those efforts (not the other way around). In order to understand that process, I had to start, analytically, with being in the world as well. This approach may be useful wherever things seem to be shifting beneath political action in ways that undermine the goals of those actions.

Related to this, how can the conceptual tools of linguistic anthropology help us understand historical moments of crisis, rupture, and collapse? In Chapter 3, this question arose as a problem of "representation." As Deaf-Blind people became blind, and access to the visual world was increasingly constrained, sighted interpreters were there to substitute that world for descriptions of it. We learned that, despite the fact that descriptions of the world can and frequently do substitute for the world, there is a limit to what language, as a means of representation, can do under conditions of existential collapse. In this context, the *limits of language* emerged as a kind of existential breaking point, felt in circumstances where talk about the world is no longer a reliable way of gaining access to, intervening in, or otherwise affecting change in the world. While this book has focused on representation via language-use and, more specifically, description, reference, and depiction, one can imagine many other forms of representation that could be at issue across contexts. For example, anyone who spent most of their time at home during the COVID-19 pandemic may have encountered, at some point, a sense that digital representations of social life were extinguishing their own capacity to substitute for social life. In this book, I have argued that there is a careful balance that must be maintained between propositional claims about the world, on the one hand, and non-propositional modes of interpretation, which make those claims necessary, urgent, and meaningful, on the other hand. The conceptual framework elaborated in this book will be of use to anyone working or living in places where crisis, collapse, or rupture disturb that balance.

Another question addressed in this book: What is the relationship between speaking a particular language and perceiving the world in a particular way? In Chapters 5 and 6, I address this question by analyzing moments when in order to express or interpret an utterance effectively the speaker had to *be* in the environment in a particular way. Linguistic anthropologists have picked up on aspects of this, building on ideas like Bourdieu's (1972) notion of "habitus," Goffman's (1964) approach to situated interaction, Merleau-Ponty's (2006 [1945]) understanding of embodiment, and the many works that have addressed the relation of language to identity. However, this case brings being and speaking, as distinct forms of semiosis, into stark relief—analyzing each in a separate moment, before the relation between them is examined. In routine circumstances, we keep them in balance, integrate them, and substitute them for one another. The analysis presented in this book shows, however, that this can't always be taken for granted in a world prone to collapse.

In Chapter 6, I also return to the conceptual frameworks linguistic anthropologists have created for thinking about the roles we take up in interaction, how they are structured, and what forms of meaning those structures generate. I recount a debate about whether the roles of "speaker" and "addressee" can be decomposed into a finite set of composite features that can be used to derive all possible participant roles found in interaction. Following Irvine (1996), I begin instead with the basic categories of "speaker" and "addressee" and ask how those categories are embedded in more specific, context-dependent role relations. Among DeafBlind people at Gallaudet University, I found that architectural structures were created explicitly to support specific participant roles. In order to account for that fact, I extended Goffman's (1981) notion of "lamination" beyond interaction into the environments created to support interaction.

Finally, as I discussed in Chapter 1, there is a long tradition among anthropologists, linguists, and philosophers of thinking about language in terms of its capacity for making claims about the world which can, through a kind of propositional reasoning, be deemed true or false. This process coordinates beliefs, perceptions, and memories with normative ways of speaking and acting to yield certain tendencies in making and evaluating such claims. However, as others have pointed out before me, the particulars of those tendencies depend on who you are. There is no universal set of "rules" or "conditions" under which some proposition or another will always be true. This book has drawn attention to the fact that in times of rapid historical change, options for who you can be—the forms of personhood available to you—may be terminally restricted. Where this is the case, language can exhaust its own capacities as a tool for action in, and on, the world. When that happens, arguments for rights and resources will carry no weight. Statements will no longer be treated as "true" or "false." Any attempt to spin things will only drive you deeper into the problems you are trying to escape. Eventually, you will realize that there is nothing more to say; no one out there is going to help you. And, yet, if there is one thing we learn from the protactile movement, it is this: In precisely this moment, when everything has fallen apart, and existence is at stake, we can turn toward one another, feel around for whatever has been left behind, and find a new way forward.

References

Bahan, Benjamin. 2009. "Sensory Orientation." *Deaf Studies Digital Journal* 1.
Barthes, R., Howard, R., & Barthes, R. (1984). *The rustle of language* (1. California paperback print., [Nachdr.]). University of California Press.
Battison, Robbin. 1978. *Lexical Borrowing in American Sign Language*. Silver Spring, MD: Linstock Press.
Bauman, Hansel. 2014. "DeafSpace: An Architecture toward a More Livable and Sustainable World." In *Deaf Gain: Raising the Stakes of Human Diversity*, edited by H-Dirksen, L. Bauman, and Joseph Murray, 375–401. Minneapolis: University of Minnesota Press.
Behm, Derick. 2019. "DEAFSPACE IN URBAN PLANNING: A Framework for Equity and Inclusion in Washington, DC." Georgetown University.
Benjamin, Walter. 1999. *The Arcades Project*. Translated by Howard Eiland. Cambridge, MA: Harvard University Press.
Boas, Franz. 1889. "On Alternating Sounds." *American Anthropologist* 2 (1): 47–54.
Bourdieu, Pierre. 1970. "The Berber House or the World Reversed." *Social Science Information* 9 (2): 151–170.
Bourdieu, Pierre. 1972. *Outline of a Theory of Practice*. Cambridge: Cambridge University Press.
Bühler, Karl. 1934. *Theory of Language: The Representational Function of Language*. Amsterdam; Philadelphia, PA: John Benjamins.
Checchetto, Alessandra, Carlo Geraci, Carlo Cecchetto, and Sandro Zucchhi. 2018. "The Language Instinct in Extreme Circumstances: The Transition to Tactile Italian Sign Language (LISt) by Deafblind Signers." *Glossa: A Journal of General Linguistics* 3 (1): 1–28. https://doi.org/10.5334/gjgl.357.
Cheng, Qi, Austin Roth, Eric Halgren, and Rachel I. Mayberry. 2019. "Effects of Early Language Deprivation on Brain Connectivity: Language Pathways in Deaf Native and Late First-Language Learners of American Sign Language." *Frontiers in Human Neuroscience* 13. https://doi.org/10.3389/fnhum.2019.00320/full.
Chomsky, Noam. 1988 [1965]. *Aspects of the Theory of Syntax*. 20. Special Technical Report / Massachusetts Institute of Technology, Research Laboratory of Electronics 11. Cambridge, MA: MIT Press.
Clark, John Lee. 2014. "Pro-Tactile: Bursting the Bubble." In *Where I Stand: On the Signing Community and My DeafBlind Experience*. Minneapolis: Handtype Press.
Clark, John Lee. 2015. "Metatactile Knowledge." *Journal of Disability Poetry and Literature* 1 (1–13): 3.
Clark, John Lee. 2017. "Distantism (Https://Johnleeclark.Tumblr.Com/)." https://johnleeclark.tumblr.com/.
Clark, John Lee. 2021. "Against Access." *Timothy McSweeney's Literary Concern* August (64).
Clark, John Lee, and Jelica B. Nuccio. 2020. "Protactile Linguistics: Discussing Recent Research Findings." *Journal of American Sign Languages and Literatures*. https://journalofasl.com/protactile-linguistics/.
Collins, Steven. 2004. "Adverbial Morphemes in Tactile American Sign Language." Graduate College of Union Institute and University.
Collins, Steven, and Karen Petronio. 1998. "What Happens in Tactile ASL?" In *Pinky Extension and Eye Gaze: Language Use in Deaf Communities*, edited by Ceil Lucas, 18–37. Washington, D.C.: Gallaudet University Press.

DeBois, John W. 1987. "Meaning without Intention: Lessons from Divination." *IPrA Papers in Pragmatics* 1 (2): 80–122. https://doi.org/10.1075/iprapip.1.2.04boi.

Djordjević, Ivana. 1993. "Objectively Speaking." *Journal of the Society of Architectural Historians* 52 (1): 59–67. https://doi.org/10.2307/990757.

Dudis, Paul G. 2004. "Body Partitioning and Real-Space Blends." *Cognitive Linguistics* 15 (2): 223–238. https://doi.org/10.1515/cogl.2004.009.

Duranti, Alessandro. 1984. *Intentions, Self, and Local Theories of Meaning: Social Action in a Samoan Context*. La Jolla, CA: Center for Human Information Processing, University of California, San Diego.

Duranti, Alessandro. 2010. "Husserl, Intersubjectivity, and Anthropology." *Anthropological Theory* 10 (1): 1–20.

Duranti, Alessandro, and Nicco A. La Mattina. 2022. "The Semiotics of Cooperation." *Annual Review of Anthropology* 51 (1): 85–101. https://doi.org/10.1146/annurev-anthro-041420-103556.

Edwards, Terra. 2014. "Language Emergence in the Seattle DeafBlind Community." Berkeley, California: University of California, Berkeley.

Edwards, Terra. 2015. "Bridging the Gap between DeafBlind Minds: Interactional and Social Foundations of Intention Attribution in the Seattle DeafBlind Community." *Frontiers in Psychology (Language Sciences Section)* 6. https://doi.org/10.3389/fpsyg.2015.01497.

Edwards, Terra. 2017. "Sign Creation in the Seattle DeafBlind Community: A Triumphant Story about the Regeneration of Obviousness." *Gesture* 16 (2): 304–327. https://doi.org/10.1075/gest.16.2.06edw.

Edwards, Terra. 2018. "Re-channeling Language: The Mutual Restructuring of Language and Infrastructure at Gallaudet University." *Journal of Linguistic Anthropology* 28 (3): 273–291.

Edwards, Terra, and Diane Brentari. 2020. "Feeling Phonology: The Emergence of Tactile Phonological Patterns in Protactile Communities in the United States." *Language* 96 (4): 819–840.

Edwards, Terra, and Diane Brentari. 2021. "The Grammatical Incorporation of Demonstratives in an Emerging Tactile Language." *Frontiers in Psychology* 11 (579992). https://doi.org/10.3389/fpsyg.2020.579992.

Edwards, Terra, and Diane Brentari. In preparation. *Language Emergence*.

Gibson, James J. 2015 [1977]. *The Ecological Approach to Visual Perception*. New York: Taylor and Francis.

Goffman, Erving. 1964. "The Neglected Situation." *American Anthropologist* 66: 133–136.

Goffman, Erving. 1981. *Footing: Forms of Talk*. Oxford: Basil Blackwell.

Goodwin, Charles. 2007. "Participation, Stance and Affect in the Org." *Discourse and Society* 18 (1): 53–73.

Goodwin, Charles. 2017. *Co-operative Action*. 1st ed. Cambridge: Cambridge University Press. https://doi.org/10.1017/9781139016735.

Goodwin, Marjorie Harness. 2017. *Haptic Sociality*. Vol. 1. Oxford: Oxford University Press. https://doi.org/10.1093/acprof:oso/9780190210465.003.0004.

Goodwin, Marjorie Harness, and Asta Cekaite. 2018. *Embodied Family Choreography: Practices of Control, Care, and Mundane Creativity*. 1st ed. New York: Routledge, 2018. https://doi.org/10.4324/9781315207773.

granda, aj, and Jelica Nuccio. 2018. "Protactile Principles." *Tactile Communications*. https://www.tactilecommunications.org/ProTactilePrinciples.

Hanks, William F. 1990. *Referential Practice: Language and Lived Space among the Maya*. Chicago: University of Chicago Press.

Hanks, William F. 2009. "Fieldwork on Deixis." *Journal of Pragmatics* 41: 10–24. https://doi.org/10.1016/j.pragma.2008.09.003.

Hanks, William F. 2013. "Counterparts: Co-presence and Ritual Intersubjectivity." *Language & Communication* 33: 263–277.
Hull, Matthew. 2012. *Government of Paper: The Materiality of Bureaucracy in Urban Pakistan*. Berkeley: University of California Press.
Irvine, Judith. 1996. "Shadow Conversations: The Indeterminacy of Participant Roles Isbn." In *Natural Histories of Discourse*, edited by Michael Silverstein and Greg Urban 131–159. Chicago: University of Chicago Press.
Iwasaki, Shimako, Meredith Barlett, Howard Manns, and Louisa Willooughby. 2018. "The Challenges of Multimodality and Multisensorality: Methodological Issues in Analyzing Tactile Signed Interaction." *Journal of Pragmatics* 143: 215–227. https://doi.org/10.1016/j.pragma.2018.05.003.
Johnson, Najma. 2020. "Najma's Addressing DB Autonomy Video." https://www.youtube.com/watch?v=D4Q_0aJenSs.
Keane, Webb. 2014. "Affordances and Reflexivity in Ethical Life: An Ethnographic Stance." *Anthropological Theory* 14 (1): 3–26. https://doi.org/10.1177/1463499614521721.
Keating, Elizabeth, and Eugene Mirus. 2003. "American Sign Language in Virtual Space: Interactions between Deaf Users of Computer-Mediated Video Communication and the Impact of Technology on Language Practices." *Language in Society* 32 (5): 693–714.
Kehler, Andrew. 2000. "Coherence and the Resolution of Ellipsis." *Linguistics and Philosophy* 23 (6): 533–575.
Klima, Edward S., and Ursula Bellugi. 1979. *The Signs of Language*. London: Harvard University Press.
Kockelman, Paul. 2005. "The Semiotic Stance." *Semiotica* 2005 (157): 233–304. https://doi.org/10.1515/semi.2005.2005.157.1-4.233.
Kockelman, Paul. 2006a. "Residence in the World: Affordances, Instruments, Actions, Roles, and Identities." *Semiotica* 162 (1/4): 19–71.
Kockelman, Paul. 2006b. "Representations of the World: Memories, Perceptions, Beliefs, Intentions, and Plans." *Semiotica* 2006 (162). https://doi.org/10.1515/SEM.2006.074.
Koestler, Frances A. 2004. *The Unseen Minority: A Social History of Blindness in the United States*. New York: AFB Press.
Kusters, Annelies. 2015. *Deaf Space in Adamorobe: An Ethnographic Study in a Village in Ghana*. Washington, D.C.: Gallaudet University Press.
Levinson, Stephen C., and Judity Holler. 2014. "The Origin of Human Multi-modal Communication." *Philosophical Transactions B* 369 (1651). https://doi.org/10.1098/rstb.2013.0302.
Lynch, Kevin. 1960. *The Image of the City*. Cambridge: Cambridge University Press.
MacCleery, Rachel, and Jonathan Tar. 2012. "NoMa: The Neighborhood That Transit Built." *Urban Land Magazine*. https://urbanland.uli.org/development-business/noma-the-neighborhood-that-transit-built/.
Malzkuhn, Matthew. 2007. "Home Customization: Understanding Deaf Ways of Being." Unpublished MA thesis. Gallaudet University.
McMillen, Sarah K. 2015. "Is Protactile Habitable at Gallaudet University: What Does It Take?" Washington, D.C.: Gallaudet University.
McNeill, David. 2005. *Gesture and Thought*. Chicago and London: Univeristy of Chicago Press.
McNeill, David, and Susan D. Duncan. 2000. "Growth Points in Thinking-for-Speaking." In *Language and Gesture*, edited by David McNeill, 1st ed., 141–161. Cambridge: Cambridge University Press. https://doi.org/10.1017/CBO9780511620850.010.
Meier, Richard P. 2002. "Why Different, Why the Same? Explaining Effects and Non-effects of Modality upon Linguistic Structure in Sign and Speech." In *Modality and Structure in Signed and Spoken Languages*, edited by Richard P. Meier, Kearsy Cormier, and David Quinto-Pozos, 1–12. Cambridge: Cambridge University Press.

Merchant, Jason. 2004. "Fragments and Ellipsis." *Linguistics and Philosophy* 27: 661–738.
Merleau-Ponty, Maurice, and Colin Smith. 2006 [1945]. *Phenomenology of Perception: An Introduction*. Repr. Routledge Classics. London: Routledge.
Mesch, Johanna. 2001. *Tactile Sign Language: Turn Taking and Questions in Signed Conversations of Deaf-Blind People*. Hamburg: Signum.
Mesch, Johanna. 2013. "Tactile Signing with One-Handed Perception." *Sign Language Studies* 13 (2): 238–263. https://doi.org/10.1353/sls.2013.0005.
Mesch, Johanna, Eli Raanes, and Lindsay Ferrara. 2015. "Co-Forming Real Space Blends in Tactile Signed Language Dialogues." *Cognitive Linguistics* 26 (2). https://doi.org/10.1515/cog-2014-0066.
Murphy, Keith M. 2015. *Swedish Design: An Ethnography*. Expertise: Cultures and Technologies of Knowledge. Ithaca: Cornell University Press.
Panofsky, Erwin. 1973. *Gothic Architecture and Scholasticism: An Inquiry into the Analogy of the Arts, Philosophy, and Religion in the Middle Ages*. New York: Meridian.
Perniss, Pamela, Inge Zwisterlood, and Asli Ozyurek. 2011. "Does Space Structure Spatial Language? Linguistic Encoding of Space in Sign Languages." *Proceedings of the Annual Meeting of the Cognitive Science Society* 33. http://escholarship.org/uc/item/7sg78556.
Petronio, Karen, and Valerie Dively. 2006. "YES, #NO, Visibility, and Variation in ASL and Tactile ASL." *Sign Language Studies* 7: 57–98.
Quinto-Pozos, David. 2002. "Deictic Points in the Visual-Gestural and Tactile-Gestural Modalities." In *Modality and Structure in Signed and Spoken Languages*, edited by Richard P. Meier, Kearsy Cormier, and David Quinto-Pozos, 442–467. Cambridge: Cambridge University Press.
Quinto-Pozos, David, and Fey Parrill. 2015. "Signers and Co-speech Gesturers Adopt Similar Strategies for Portraying Viewpoint in Narratives." *Topics in Cognitive Science* 7: 12–35.
Rawls, Anne. 2002. "Editor's Introduction." In *Ethnomethodology's Program: Working Out Durkheim's Aphorism*, edited by Anne Rawls, 1–64. Oxford: Rowman & Littlefield.
Reed, Charlotte M., Lorraine A. Delhorne, Nathaniel I. Durlach, and Susan D. Fischer. 1995. "A Study of the Tactual Reception of Sign Language." *Journal of Speech and Hearing Research* 38: 477–489.
Rochester, Junius. 2004. *Seattle's Best-Kept Secret: A History of the Lighthouse for the Blind, Inc.: Celebrating Ninety Years*. Seattle: Tommie Press.
Romilus, Yashaira, and Jasper Norman. n.d. "Protactile Theatre." *PTT* (blog). http://protactiletheatre.org/.
Rosaldo, Michelle. n.d. "The Things We Do with Words: Ilongot Speech Acts and Speech Act Theory in Philosophy." *Language in Society* 11 (2): 203–237. http://www.jstor.org/stable/4167311.
Rutherford, Danilyn. 2022. "Proprioceptive Sociality." Conference Presentation, Department of Anthropology, University of Chicago, October 3, 2022.
Sandler, Wendy. 2013. "Dedicated Gestures and the Emergence of Sign Language." *Gesture* 12 (3): 265–307.
Sangalang, Jordan. 2012. "Privacy in DeafSpace." Unpublished MA thesis. Gallaudet University.
Sapir, Edward. 1995 [1934]. "The Grammarian and His Language." In *Selected Writings of Edward Sapir in Language, Culture, and Personality*, edited by David Mandelbaum, 564–568. Berkeley: University of California Press.
Saussure, Ferdinand de. 1972 [1915]. *Course in General Linguistics*. New York: McGraw Hill.
Scott, Robert A. 1981. *The Making of Blind Men: A Study of Adult Socialization*. 1st paperback ed. New Brunswick, NJ: Transaction Books.
Searle, John. 1983. *Intentionality*. Cambridge: Cambridge University Press.
Shopen, Timothy. 1973. "Elipsis as Grammatical Indeterminacy." *Foundations of Language* 10 (1): 65–77. https://www.jstor.org/stable/25000705.

Sidnell, Jack. 2015. "Conversation Analysis." In *The Oxford Handbook of Linguistic Analysis*, edited by Bernd Heine and Heiko Narrog. Oxford: Oxford University Press.

Silverstein, Michael. 1976. "Shifters, Linguistic Categories, and Cultural Description." In *Meaning in Anthropology*, edited by Keith Basso and Henry A. Selby, 11–55. Albuquerque, NM: University of New Mexico Press.

Silverstein, Michael. 2019. "Texts, Entextualized and Artifactualized: The Shapes of Discourse." *College English* 82 (1): 55–76.

Simmel, G. (1971). *On individuality and social forms: Selected writings* (D. N. Levine, Ed.; Nachdr.). Univ. of Chicago Press.

Sirvage, Robert T., dir. 2015. *Measuring the Immeasurable: The Legacy of Atomization and Dorsality as a Pathway in Making Deaf Epistemology Quantifiable—An Insight from DeafSpace*. https://www.youtube.com/watch?v=EPTrOO6EYCY.

Sirvage, Robert T., dir. 2017. "Access & Exposure in Deaf Space Design."

Slobin, Dan I. 1996. "From 'Thought and Language' to 'Thinking for Speaking'." In *Rethinking Linguistic Relativity*, edited by John J. Gumperz and Stephen C. Levinson, 70–96. Cambridge: Cambridge University Press.

Smith, T. B. (2002). GUIDELINES: Practical Tips for Working and Socializing with Deaf-Blind People. *Interpreting*, 8. https://digitalcommons.wou.edu/dbi_interpreters/8.

Stokoe, William C. 1960. "Sign Language Structure: An Outline of the Visual Communication Systems of the American Deaf." *Journal of Deaf Studies and Deaf Education* 10.

Throop, C. Jason. 2016. "Aspects, Affordances, Breakdowns: Some Phenomenological Anthropological Reflections on Webb Keane's *Ethical Life: Its Natural and Social Histories*." *HAU: Journal of Ethnographic Theory* 6 (1): 469–475. https://doi.org/10.14318/hau6.1.026.

Van Cleve, John V., ed. 2007. *The Deaf History Reader*. Washington, D.C.: Gallaudet University Press.

Weiss, Erica, and Carole McGranahan. 2021. "Rethinking Pseudonyms in Ethnography: An Introduction." *American Ethnologist Website* (blog). https://americanethnologist.org/features/collections/rethinking-pseudonyms-in-ethnography/rethinking-pseudonyms-in-ethnography-an-introduction.

Willoughby, Louisa, Shimako Iwasaki, Meredith Bartlett, and Howard Manns. 2018. "Tactile Sign Languages." In *Handbook of Pragmatics*, edited by Jan-Ola Östman and Jef Verschueren, 21:239–258. Amsterdam: Benjamins.

Index

Abused Deaf Women's Advocacy Service (ADWAS) 76
access 6–7, 31, 37–39, 42, 46, 72–74, 83, 109, 131, 133–134
 sensory 127, 130
 tactile 14, 26–27, 38, 46, 99, 115–116
accommodation 19, 36, 52, 58, 59, 63, 76
actions 15–16, 19–20, 48, 50–53, 56, 59, 61, 63–65, 68–69, 73, 81, 89, 91, 92, 96, 99–100, 107–108, 116–117, 138, 140
addressee (participant role) 29, 33, 42, 93–94, 100, 116–119, 123, 132, 139
Adrijana 4, 8, 129
 leadership in DeafBlind community 1, 3, 9, 27, 46–47, 75–79, 83–99, 109–110
 life history 36–37, 50, 61
 protactile perspective of 17, 21–23, 25–26, 61, 63, 72, 90, 95, 112–119
affective responses 64–65, 70
affordances 29–30, 33, 92, 108, 124, 135, 138
 building 125, 131, 132
 in Deaf Space 130–131
 interpreting 19, 20, 89, 96, 98, 114
 residential whole and 15–17, 48–53, 81–82, 107
 starting with 56–58, 82, 96, 116–117
 tactile 2, 100, 111, 113–114, 130
 visual 71, 113–114
air space 7, 27–28, 117, 129
AI 44–45
Amanda 95–97
American Sign Language (ASL) 1, 8, 37, 38–42, 45, 47, 55, 65, 67, 71, 75, 76, 84, 87, 88, 100, 105–106, 112, 122, 126, 131
 challenges for DeafBlind people 7, 26–27, 29, 31–33, 60–62, 72, 83, 92, 114, 127–128
Americans with Disabilities Act 49, 55
animator 67, 123
Ann 49
anti-tactility 6, 25, 42
appropriateness (normative behavior) 4, 18, 42, 65–66, 71, 100, 138 (*see also* norms, politeness)

appropriateness (to environment) 14, 15, 52, 59–60, 63, 68, 73, 83, 91, 112, 116, 120 (*see also* effectiveness)
architecture 119, 120, 124–127, 130–131, 135, 139 (*see also* Deaf Space)
articulators 27–28, 114
attention 33–34, 71, 95, 118, 128
Auslan 27
author (participant role) 67, 123
autonomy 100–101

Bahan, Ben 125, 131
Barthes, Roland 70
Bauman, Dirksen 131
being
 here, there 10, 15, 16, 103, 116
 in the world 1, 4, 12, 16, 19, 21, 34, 60, 83, 100, 114, 118, 128, 137–138 (*see also* residence in the world)
being for speaking 104, 111–118
benches 124–125, 131
blindfolds 25, 89, 115
Boas, Franz 104–106
Boeing 36, 38
Bourdieu, Pierre 139
Braille 6–7, 20, 23, 24–25, 41–42, 49, 54, 99, 117
Brentari, Diane 27, 28
bridge-building 40–42

Cartesian space 19–20
channels 6, 27–30, 90, 97–99, 116–117, 135
Charlotte 4, 10–11, 13–17, 23, 24, 30–31, 131–132
Clark, John Lee 2, 5–8, 23–24, 28, 133–134
co-articulation 27–28
co-existence 121, 133–135
collapse 1, 9, 34, 38, 48, 50, 53, 59, 70–71, 73, 83, 138–140
 cycles of 49, 52, 56
 signs of 52, 57, 64, 69, 73–74
commitment 21–23, 52, 64–67, 69–70, 73, 104, 114

community
  Deaf 39, 49, 108, 109, 120–122, 126
  DeafBlind 2–5, 9, 10, 14, 17, 26–27, 35, 38, 41–43, 45–47, 48, 50, 52–54, 56, 58, 59, 63, 67–68, 70, 75, 77–79, 81–82, 85, 86, 99–100, 103, 108–110, 119, 121, 137
competence 137
conceptualization 106
contact space 6, 28
contextualization 15–16, 25, 48, 51, 64, 116, 116–118
coordination 28, 68, 132
co-presence 95–96, 116, 117–118, 120, 138
COVID-19 138
curb-cuts 31–33, 127–129

Dawn 40–41
Deaf culture 47, 87, 122
Deaf esthetic 126
Deaf floors 130–131
Deaf Space 119, 120–122, 124–127, 130–132, 134–136
Deaf world 51, 61
DeafBlind Friendly Zone 77, 85
DeafBlind Service Center (DBSC) 9, 24, 38, 42–46, 75–79, 83–88, 90, 109–110, 119
deictics (*see* deixis)
de-institutionalization (*see* integration)
deixis 33–34, 102, 103–104, 107, 112–115, 118–119, 128–129
demonstrative 119
denial 17, 53–56, 60–62
denotational text 137
Department of Services for the Blind (DSB) 41–42, 44–45, 49, 85
description (*see* representation of the world; interpreters: describing world)
design 5, 32, 120–122, 124–135 (*see also* architecture, Deaf Space)
direct perception 18–19
distantism 63
dorsality 126

eddies 134
efficacy 1, 11, 13, 15, 16, 58–60, 63, 68, 69, 73, 83, 91, 100, 112, 116, 138
Elliot 19
ellipsis 11–12
embodiment 139
empathic processes 126

employment 17, 35, 39, 41, 46, 93, 111
energetic response 65, 70
English 7, 8, 12, 39, 42, 67, 96, 100, 105–106, 107
environment 2, 5, 10, 12, 13, 23, 31, 34, 38, 41, 44, 46, 56, 59, 65, 69, 78, 81, 83, 89, 91, 102, 103, 116, 117, 122, 124, 129, 130–131 (*see also* deixis)
  affordances interpreted within 15–20, 24–25, 30, 32–33, 70–71, 82, 92, 96, 107–108, 119, 138
  affordances provided by 16–20, 50, 56–58, 111–114
  blind 36
  channeling of 90, 98–100
  Deaf 37, 41, 76, 96, 126
  hearing 36–37, 61, 96
  lamination of 121, 133–135, 139
  obstacles in 131
  protactile 4, 6, 26–27, 42, 77, 97–98, 101, 119, 129
  response to 125
  sighted 34, 71
  structures 119, 125–126, 128, 132
existential crisis 16–17, 34, 51, 87, 138–139
existential strain 52, 59, 73

feedback 95, 97–98, 116
feeling for relations 65, 106
Felicia 60–61
fingerspelling 39, 46, 96, 108
form-feeling 106
Frank 126
freezing 77–79

Gallaudet University 31–32, 40, 119, 120–122, 124, 129, 131–134, 136, 139
George 41, 95, 97
gesture 29, 37, 105–107
Gibson, James J. 16, 18–19, 30, 56–58
Glen 49–50
Goffman, Erving 115, 123, 139
going tactile 60–63, 88–89, 94, 99, 110, 113, 132
grammatical categories 103, 105–106, 114, 119, 128
grammatical structure 27, 29–31, 102, 103, 104, 106, 113, 118, 128
granda, aj 5, 27
grief 9, 17

habit 4, 15, 64, 67, 77, 81, 96, 100–101, 106, 107, 122, 126, 130
habitus 139
Hall, Edward T. 58
Heidegger, Martin 107–108
Helen 17–18, 68–71, 79–82
Henry 121, 127, 130, 134
homogenization 52, 57–58, 93

identity 5, 15, 48, 49, 50–52, 56, 58–59, 64, 69, 73, 81, 89, 100, 102, 114, 139–140 (*see also* residential whole)
  DeafBlind 46–47, 53–54, 60–61, 81, 83, 100, 109
imagistic-categorial synthesis 106–107
inclusion 6, 84, 133 (*see also* accommodation)
incorporation 15–16, 27, 29, 48, 51, 64, 111, 117–118, 130–132
inference 19, 21–23, 25, 42, 51, 73, 99
information 3, 17, 42, 78, 89, 112, 115, 117, 130–131, 135
  environmental 10, 44, 130
  source 9, 18, 90, 92, 118
  tactile 20, 25, 116
infrastructure 43, 53, 119, 120 (*see also* architecture, Deaf Space)
instruments 15–16, 48, 50, 59, 64, 71, 81, 92, 100, 107
integration 36
intentionality 21–22
interaction 5, 9, 13, 22, 25, 27, 30, 37–38, 57, 71, 94, 115, 116, 119, 123, 126, 137, 139
interactional text 137
interpretant 64
interpreters 3, 8–10, 19, 39–47, 49, 51, 53, 55, 69, 78, 84, 87–90, 91–92, 109–110, 111, 114, 115, 120, 126
  communication between DeafBlind people and 28, 60, 63, 66–67, 83–84, 94, 96
  dependence on 1, 23, 28, 43–44, 61–62, 81–82, 84, 100
  describing world 13, 17, 23, 30–31, 70–73, 81, 111, 118, 138
intuition 42, 78, 83, 92, 94, 96–98, 100, 106, 110, 117
Irvine, Judith 123–124, 139
isolation 3, 17, 36–37, 51, 53, 62, 66, 85, 87, 88, 110 (*see also* loneliness)

Janet 24, 53, 59
Jeff 24
Jodi 75, 83
Joey 39
Johnson, Najma 5, 100–101
Julie 65

Kathryn 54–55, 59
Ken 97
Kirk 19–20
Kockelman, Paul 15, 21, 48, 107

lamination 119, 121, 123–124, 133–135, 139
language emergence 25–31, 34, 84, 102, 113, 118, 128, 138
language learning 25, 39, 104–105, 119, 129
language planning 27
langue 137
Laura 40
leadership problem 86
Leah 43–44
Lee 1, 3, 4, 17, 27, 59, 61–63, 71–72, 75–76, 82, 83, 88–89, 94–98, 99, 110, 112, 115, 116, 117, 118, 119, 129
Levinson, Stephen 123–124
Lighthouse for the Blind 35–46, 54, 62, 76, 84, 110, 115
limits of language 1, 2, 10, 14, 15, 20, 31–32, 34, 70, 137, 138
locative 113, 119
loneliness 17, 37, 88 (*see also* isolation)
Louise 87
Lynn 97

mainstreaming (*see* integration)
Mansfield, Dan 42–43, 45
mapping (direction-giving) 129
McDermot, Jim 44–45
mediation 28, 41–42, 47, 63, 74, 83, 90, 94, 96, 100, 110, 134 (*see also* accommodation, interpreters)
memory 26, 31, 52, 72, 73, 139
Merleau-Ponty 139
metatactile knowledge 23–28
modality 30, 39, 97
  sensory 27, 29, 32
  tactile 28, 76
motor lines 114
Murphy, Keith 126

mutual monitoring 115–116, 135 (*see also* co-presence; feedback; protactile sitting)

naturalization 84–85, 89
niche 57
non-propositional semiosis 13, 19–20, 73–74, 138, 139
norms 16, 21, 52, 58, 59, 64, 76, 79, 89, 91–92, 139–140
  Deaf 76–77, 97
  protactile 3, 25, 96, 120, 133
  sighted 2, 9, 14, 18, 25, 34, 47, 49, 61, 63, 65, 71, 83, 97, 100, 109, 120
  white 101
North of Massachusetts Avenue (NoMa) 121–122
Nuccio, Jelica 5, 27

Oliver 26

Palasmaa, Juhani 126–127
parole 137
participation
  framework 66–67, 118, 123–124, 132, 135, 139
  protactile structures of 132
passive seeing 71
path 113, 119, 129
performance 137
Philip 31–34, 127, 129
pointing 5, 27, 29, 32–33, 94, 103, 107, 111–112, 114
politics 4, 5, 19, 20, 24, 36, 102, 103, 108, 110, 137
  activism and organizing 30, 34, 42–46, 138
  DeafBlind 2, 47, 53, 81, 83
  protactile 119
predication 11–12, 22
propositionality 11–15, 20, 22, 73, 138–140
proprioception 22, 28–29, 113, 117, 135
protactile 32, 76–77, 93, 95–96, 98, 110–111, 115, 116, 128
protactile design 132–133
protactile language 8, 25, 27–31, 34, 42, 100–101, 113–114, 118, 128–129
protactile movement 2, 3, 5, 12, 18, 19, 21, 24–25, 47, 52, 59, 73–74, 104, 112, 134, 138, 140

beginnings of 60, 75, 83, 89, 92, 99–102, 103, 110–111, 118–119, 137
Gallaudet and 120–121, 127, 133
period prior to 7, 13, 23, 26, 30–31, 60, 63, 73, 90, 99, 111, 115, 116
protactile people 6, 8, 27, 93, 96, 98, 102, 103, 110–111, 113–114, 117, 119, 131–132, 135
protactile practices 46, 96–97, 132–133
protactile sitting 94–96
protactile space 134
protactile theory 47, 73, 100, 102, 112, 120, 134
protactile walking 110, 132

race 100–101
reality effect 70
Rebecca 37–38
recognition 4, 30, 34, 42–45
reference 31, 33, 34, 102, 103, 107, 112, 114–115, 118–119, 129, 137–138 (*see also* deixis)
representation 29, 33, 64, 71, 90, 107, 113, 131, 134, 138 (*see also* representation of the world)
representation of the world 1, 4, 15, 18, 20–22, 25–26, 30–31, 34, 42, 69, 73, 82, 90, 92, 100, 102, 107, 118, 128, 129, 135–136, 138
representational response 64–65, 70
residence in the world 4, 15–16, 18, 20–22, 30, 34, 42, 82, 91, 102, 107, 111, 125, 128, 129, 135 (*see also* being: in the world)
residential whole 15, 48–49, 51–53, 82, 107
Robert 91
roles 3, 4, 15–16, 35–36, 61, 63, 86–87, 90, 92–93, 96, 99, 117
  participation framework 118, 123–124, 132, 139
  within residential whole 48–52, 64, 68–69, 81, 100, 107–109, 117, 138
Roman 30–31, 72, 96–97
Ronald 67
Rose 67

Sam 21–23, 26
Sapir, Edward 105–106
schemata 107, 113, 119

schools
  Deaf 1, 36–37, 49, 54
  residential 36, 49
Seattle 3, 5, 10, 14, 17, 24, 26, 28, 30–31, 35–51, 53– 56, 58– 62, 66–69, 72–73, 75–77, 79–82, 92, 101–102, 103, 104, 109, 119, 120, 131–132, 134
Seattle Central Community College 39–40, 46, 109, 115
semiosis 12, 13, 15, 21, 34, 73, 107, 137, 139 (*see also* non-propositional semiosis)
semiotics 8, 138
senior citizens 9, 85–88, 90
sensory reach 130–131
sidewalks 31–32, 126, 132 (*see also* curb-cuts)
sighted space 82, 109
sightline 113–114
sign language 8, 26, 108 (*see also* American Sign Language, Auslan, fingerspelling, protactile language, signed exact English)
signed exact English 39
Sirvage, Robert T. 124–126, 130
situation 115, 135
Slobin, Dan 106
Smith, Theresa 86
socialization 23, 36, 57–58, 108
  sighted 25, 110
Sorenson Language and Communication Center (SLCC) 124–125, 133
sound-blindness 104
space 32, 99, 112–113, 128 (*see also* air space, Cartesian space, contact space, Deaf space, protactile space, sighted space)
speaker 8, 9, 14, 28, 30, 32, 33, 64, 104, 106, 107, 116–118, 123, 128, 132, 139
standards (*see* norms)
Stokoe, William 105
Support Service Providers (SSPs) 38, 86, 88
Susan 62

tactile communication 8, 25, 42, 55, 62, 68, 75–77, 81, 83–84, 92, 93–94, 110, 111 (*see also* protactile language)
Tactile Mind Research Collaborative 133–134

tactile people 38, 46, 55, 60–61, 63, 69, 75, 89, 90, 91, 93, 98, 109–110, 115 (*see also* identity: DeafBlind)
Tactile Pictionary 99
tactile reception 7, 27, 29, 32, 42, 56, 65, 88, 127
tactile scope 72
tactile world 31, 42, 90, 101, 103
thinking for speaking 103–104
trailability 134–135
translation 8–9, 42, 107
trauma and touch 101
triangles 125
tunnel vision 46, 50, 63, 75, 108, 109, 110
  people 39, 46, 60–63, 69, 75, 89, 91, 93, 98, 99, 109
turn-taking problem 67

urban development 31, 119, 121–122, 124, 133, 135
Usher Syndrome 1, 55

Victor 114
visual analysis 71
visual communication 7, 26, 27, 28, 59, 76, 105, 108 (*see also* Sign Language, Auslan, Deaf Space, fingerspelling, signed exact English, sign language)
vocational rehabilitation 35

Washington, D.C. 1, 5, 30, 31, 119, 120, 121
Washington state government 43, 53, 81
ways of being 1, 5, 16, 31, 34, 60, 66, 68, 100, 102, 104, 107–108, 114, 118, 138 (*see also* identity)
  Deaf 125–126 (*see also* Deaf Space)
  DeafBlind 30, 35, 46, 75, 96, 100, 104, 107, 114, 115, 118 (*see also* tactile people, tunnel vision people)
  protactile 22, 102, 111, 114, 116, 119, 128
  tactile 2, 10, 25, 55, 109, 111, 118
  visual 83, 115
workshops
  interpreter 71
  protactile 3–4, 27–28, 88–95, 97–98, 110, 112, 114– 117, 129
  sheltered 35–36

The manufacturer's authorised representative in the EU for product safety is Oxford
University Press España S.A. of El Parque Empresarial San Fernando de Henares,
Avenida de Castilla, 2 – 28830 Madrid (www.oup.es/en or product.safety@oup.com).
OUP España S.A. also acts as importer into Spain of products made by the manufacturer.

Printed in the USA/Agawam, MA
April 11, 2025

885760.006